MASS VIOLENCE IN AMERICA

MASS VIOLENCE IN AMERICA

THE MASKED WAR

William J. Burns

ARNO PRESS & THE NEW YORK TIMES

New York · 1969

Editorial Note

NATIONS, LIKE MEN, ARE SOMETIMES INTERESTED IN BURYING THE PAST.

In early 1968, after more than five years marked by political assassinations, racial uprisings, campus disorders, mass demonstrations and the violent suppression of protest, *The New York Times Magazine* asked a group of distinguished scholars to reply to the question, "Is America by nature a violent society?" In answer, University of Chicago anthropologist Clifford Geertz wrote:

> "We do not know very well what kind of society we live in, what kind of history we have had, what kind of people we are. We are just now beginning to find out, the hard way . . ."

The proposition was astonishing but correct: what was least understood about domestic political violence was its role in American history. It was common knowledge that the United States had had a Revolution, a Civil War, some trouble with the Indians and a period of labor-management conflict. But one could search the shelves of the nation's great libraries without discovering more than a handful of works on the subject of violence in American history, and these hopelessly out of date.

Historians had generally ignored or soft-pedaled the history of farmer uprisings, native vigilantism, labor-management struggles, ethnic conflicts and race riots; comparative work in the history of social conflict was particularly weak. Sociologists and political scientists in the grip of "consensus" theory tended to treat episodes of mass violence in America as insignificant or aberrational—temporary exceptions to the norm of peaceful progress. Psychologists and behavioral scientists discussed "mob violence" in terms which suggested that riots, revolts, insurrections and official violence were the products of individual or group pathology. All such interpretations had the effect not only of minimizing group violence in America, but of depriving it of political content—hence, of relevance to the present.

As a result, as late as 1968, the rich, multifarious and often terrifying history of domestic political violence was still largely *terra incognita*. So long as most Americans wished to keep certain skeletons locked away in their closets, few scholars would attempt to open doors. Conversely, once the American people, frightened yet emboldened by the sudden reappearance of intense social conflict, began to ask new questions about the past, so did the scholars.

Our purpose in helping Arno Press and *The New York Times* select and publish significant documents in the history of political violence has not been to compound past errors by overemphasizing the role of conflict in American history. On the contrary, our aim has been to provide materials which will aid in the search for an accurate perspective on the present. MASS VIOLENCE IN AMERICA includes eyewitness reports, government documents and other descriptive and analytic material relating to mass political violence in the United States. These documents not only provide information—they give the "feel" or "flavor" of past eras of civil disorder by evoking the emotional and political context in which revolts took place. Most of them have long been out of print and are obtainable, if at all, only in the nation's largest libraries.

The scope of this series is wide, ranging from accounts of Indian warfare to descriptions of labor-management violence, from narratives of colonial insurrections to reports on modern racial uprisings. It is not, however, limitless, nor were the constituent volumes carelessly selected. The principle of coherence which guided the selections is implicit in the phrase "mass political violence." "Mass" denotes activity engaged in by large groups rather than individuals acting alone; "political" suggests a relationship between such activity and competition among domestic groups for power, property and prestige; and "violence" is narrowly construed as resulting in physical damage to persons or property. In short, the materials reproduced herein are intended to illuminate the resort to violence by American groups seeking to change or to preserve the status quo. Although historical, they are of interest to any who wishes to understand the causes, nature and direction of domestic political violence, whether they be social scientists, historians or just interested Americans.

Of course, we are particularly hopeful that these volumes will prove useful to those now engaged in curriculum-revision and the teaching of high school and college courses in the area of American studies. What Christopher Jencks and David Reisman term "the Academic Revolution" has made difficult demands on all educators, not the least of which is the demand for courses which are both relevant to the condition of modern America and of the highest academic quality. These volumes are meant to provide raw material for such courses—primary source matter which will help both instructors and students to deepen and enrich their views of the American experience.

Most important, the editors and publisher recognize that these volumes appear during a national crisis which is also a crisis of the spirit, a time in which the public response to various manifestations of civil disorder is increasingly governed by anger, fear and hysteria. In such an atmosphere it is important to recognize that one is not alone in time—that such events have taken place before in America and, unless fundamental changes in our social and political life take place, will probably recur in the future. Our fondest hope is that this work, and others like it, will help to keep alive, in a time of growing unreason, the spirit of reasoned inquiry.

RICHARD E. RUBENSTEIN
The Adlai Stevenson Institute
Chicago, Illinois

ROBERT M. FOGELSON
Harvard-MIT Joint Center
for Urban Studies
Cambridge, Massachusetts

THE MASKED WAR

WILLIAM J. BURNS

THE
MASKED WAR

THE STORY OF A PERIL THAT THREATENED
THE UNITED STATES BY THE MAN WHO
UNCOVERED THE DYNAMITE CON-
SPIRATORS AND SENT THEM
TO JAIL

BY

WILLIAM J. BURNS

NEW YORK
GEORGE H. DORAN COMPANY

CONTENTS

CONTENTS

THE MASKED WAR

CHAPTER I

THE BETRAYAL OF LABOR TO ANARCHY

In order that this story may not seem utterly incredible to the great majority of American citizens who take life complacently, depending entirely on the machine of government to look after their safety and welfare, I shall give them assurance in the first paragraph that they shall find in this volume full proof for each of the startling facts narrated, giving for the first time the evidence I gathered against John J. McNamara, James B. McNamara and the conspirators of their union who were convicted at Indianapolis.

The evidence did not come out at the trials of the McNamaras, for they pleaded guilty to murder. As I look back over my diary and the reports of my operatives it seems strange to me that men at the head of a once powerful labor organization could have worked hand in glove with Anarchists to murder and destroy for a series of years, fool the honest workmen supporting the union,

9

and evade the penalty of the law for their crimes.

There are, perhaps, scores of people who will read this story and who would rather read my death notice. I do not say that there are hundreds or thousands who would slay me, but I do know of those who tried their best to eliminate me. So far as I am concerned—and I am now fifty-two years old—they have failed, but these same people have taken the lives of over a hundred other human beings. I have brought a number of them to justice, and I am still alive and watchful for my own safety. My name is William J. Burns, and my address is New York, London, Paris, Montreal, Chicago, San Francisco, Los Angeles, Seattle, New Orleans, Boston, Philadelphia, Cleveland, and wherever else a law-abiding citizen may find need of men who know how to go quietly about throwing out of ambush a hidden assassin or drawing from cover criminals who prey upon those who walk straight.

It will be well for honest, clean-living working-men with a family, a craft and a spark of patriotism in them to read the reports of my operatives as they gradually unfold the story of anarchy, for then they will come to know by actual evidence the nature and quality of those in whom they have put their trust as leaders and to whom they have given week after week a percentage of their wages. It will be more important for them to read and consider than for the employer, although there are thousands of employers who will have their eyes opened wide.

Every possible lie that could be hatched was aimed at me while my net closed on the McNamaras and those of the International Bridge and Structural Iron Workers, who betrayed the workers of that union to the Anarchists. Not only were efforts made to kill me, but every conceivable effort was made to kill my reputation. I am called the arch-enemy of organized labor. The fact is that I believe in organized labor, and believe that it has helped the workingman and will help him more when the unions shall purge themselves of such men as fight for their leadership to graft, to destroy and to kill.

The war with dynamite was a war of Anarchy against the established form of government of this country. It was masked under the cause of Labor. This is not figurative at all. It is fact. My reports of investigations among the Anarchists in this country, written in the terse and simple language of my investigators, will prove it. Personally, as well as through these reports, I know this, for I spent a part of my time trailing the Anarchists and living among them in their nest at Home Colony, near Tacoma, Wash., the community which provided two of the men who assisted J. B. McNamara in blowing up the Los Angeles Times Building and sending to a dreadful death twenty-one hard-working, innocent heads of families.

Were it not that my operatives proved of exceptional ability and in their reports gave names, addresses and dates, and that each operative was checked up by another, this book would read as a product of remarkable imagination. But the reader is not asked to take it on its face, for the same proof that would have been offered in evidence at Los Angeles will be given him just as it would have been given to the jury chosen to try the McNamaras.

J. J. McNamara, the secretary-treasurer of the International Union of Bridge and Structural Iron Workers, and his brother, J. B. McNamara, were pictured as martyrs, and great mass-meetings and parades were held by Socialists and by workingmen who were not Socialists to enlist the country's sympathy for them. An immense fund was drawn from the pockets of union men to pay Darrow and his advisers in the defense. A threat was made to call a general strike and tie up every industry in the United States so that the courts might be intimidated. A social revolution seemed at hand, but the martyrs who bring revolutions to a head are men with the good of humanity at heart, and the McNamaras were not of that kind.

When J. B. McNamara was starting for the Pacific Coast to blow up the Los Angeles Times Building his brother, J. J. McNamara, insisted on his buying a round-trip ticket so that he would save money. On another occasion, when J. B. McNamara reported at the International Headquarters in Indianapolis after exploding nitroglycerin in a non-union plant without doing any vast damage, J. J. cried with a profane utterance of the Savior's name as prefix: "Don't you know that stuff costs $1.30 a quart?" It would be hard for any man capable of the least degree of thought to picture J. J. McNamara as a martyr.

With J. B. McNamara there was no such thing as conscience. He was deep in the dregs of immoral living, as was his brother, who directed him in his tours of murder and destruction. After destroying the Los Angeles Times Building and its twenty-one occupants, he enjoyed a long carouse on a hunting trip in Wisconsin, he never expressed any remorse for his act and continued his course as if nothing had happened. He started as a boy in a childish way that landed him in a house of correction, and as a young man he debauched himself so that when he was not murdering and destroying he was drinking and pursuing women. He generally carried with him pictures so unfit that the mere mention of them is a matter to cause hesitation. There could be no stuff of martyrs in that man.

But this is not the place in the story to treat of these two labor "leaders" as specimens of criminals and degenerates. The facts are merely put forth as introductory so that the reader will be ready for the evidence as it comes along. Their actions will tell the stories of their lives. The reports of my

investigators will give the really honest and hard-
working man an idea of what they did with the
money workingmen turned in to the union, the money
their wives and children had to manage to get along
without.

CHAPTER II

ATTEMPTS TO KILL BURNS

Prior to September 4, 1910, I was considered anything but an enemy of labor. That was the date upon which I began an investigation of the men back of the reign of terror for the employers of labor in bridge and structural iron work throughout the country. A national strike of the structural iron workers had been called, back in 1905, and for five years buildings, bridges and structural supplies had been wrecked with bombs, buildings had been fired and men slugged, maimed and killed.

The employers demanded the right to employ both union and non-union labor. The union insisted that every shop and every job should be closed against workers who did not belong to the union.

It was on this date, the date of the employment of my agency, nearly a month before the destruction of the Los Angeles Times Building, that my forces were turned against the criminal "representatives" of labor. Prior to that I was in high favor with the unions, for I had been employed to uncover and bring to justice the doers of evil among the rich. The Oregon land fraud cases had been brought to a successful conclusion, and I had been called to San Francisco to clear up the graft situation there for those people who wanted corruption driven out of their municipal government. My quarry was the rich then, and I went after the rich crook just as I would go after any menace to society. Whether a crook has millions at his command or just his wits and a knife makes no difference to me. My business is to detect criminals and bring them to the courts for trial. In San Francisco, when I was after the men of wealth and long-established political power, a price was set on my head just as it was set afterward when I started to drag from their hiding places the men with torch and dynamite who fired and killed in labor's name.

These two situations, bringing about personal peril, may be interesting just at this juncture; the one coming about through the prosecution of the rich malefactor and the other through the search for the malefactors who posed as representatives of labor.

The wealthy criminals felt my net drawing closer and closer, and they seemed to realize that my elimination would help destroy that net. A man from the sub-strata of human depravity contracted with certain parties to murder five of us and to murder our chief witness, Gallagher. His price was three thousand dollars for the five lives. The deaths of Gallagher and myself would have meant the complete ruin of the chances of the prosecution for success. This assassin got busy but fortunately we

learned of his contract in time, and he was balked.
Not, however, until he had blown up Gallagher's
house. It is clearly in the recollection of the majority of newspaper readers what the next tack was.
Francis J. Heney, the special prosecutor of the graft
cases, was shot down in open court. Fortunately his
wound was not fatal, and the prosecution went right
on to a successful termination.

Some of my reports will show how, on the other
hand, those alleged representatives and apostles of
labor involved in the dynamiting outrages tried to
plant dress suit cases filled with nitroglycerin in
rooms adjoining mine at hotels, and how they
planned to blow up my offices with every one in
them. The most daring of all efforts was checked
in a way that was simple and that proved most ef-
fective.

When it was certain that the McNamaras were
doomed, when my array of witnesses to back up the
McManigal confession was scanned and found to be
frightful for the chances of the defense a certain
once eminent gentleman of the Pacific Coast—who
later came upon disgrace—let it be known that only
the withdrawal of Burns could save the accused
men.

Now this statement, coming from a man of edu-
cation and some fame, a man deeply interested in
the acquittal of the McNamaras, meant more peril
to me than all the loud-mouthed threats that might
be made in every corner saloon from Los Angeles

to New York. His suggestion would carry further
than the commands of the McNamaras themselves.
I had one of my operatives in touch with this gentleman—a fact which may cause him much surprise
and disgust. That operative, a man of high intelligence, realized in a moment what that remark
meant. It was the signal to go out and "get"
Burns. There was only one way, as I saw it, to
have that order recalled. I sent the operative back
to this gentleman to inform him that if anything
happened to me the same thing would happen to
him.

"But, my God!" cried this gentleman from his
swivel chair, "some crank might kill him! I would
not be responsible."

My operative reported to me.

With another message my representative returned to the office of the gentleman who thought
that my withdrawal was the only hope of the Mc-
Namaras.

He said:

"Mr. Blank, Mr. Burns asks me to tell you that
if he is killed by a crank another crank will kill
you."

The suggestion about my withdrawal was hurriedly recalled, and we proceeded with the selection
of a jury, that is, counsel for the prosecution and
the defense went about that work while my agency
proceeded about uncovering the attempts to bribe
jurors and talesmen as they were called.

Therefore, on September 4, 1910, I turned from hunting down wealthy criminals and began, at the request of the McClintic-Marshall Company, to hunt down the dynamiters who had carried on a masked war for five years through the United States. Another detective agency had been employed before that and had drawn a great deal of money from those companies which had suffered from these attacks in the dark. Their usual reports were to the effect that explosions had occurred at such and such places on such and such dates, and that they were being investigated. No one was arrested.

On my return to my Chicago office in the summer of 1910, after an absence of several days in New York on important matters connected with the American Bankers' Association, I was informed that our Chicago office had been called on to investigate a very important dynamiting case for the McClintic-Marshall Construction Company, of Pittsburgh. A railroad bridge at Indiana Harbor, Ind., constructed by this firm had been dynamited, and the explosion took place just before a crowded passenger train had approached it.

As I had organized the William J. Burns National Detective Agency with a view of succeeding where others failed, and having just come into the private detective business, I felt that we should do more than make a merely perfunctory investigation on important matters of this character. Therefore,

I sent for the operative who made the investigation, and questioned him as to what he had accomplished. In reply he stated, in a great deal of language, that he had proceeded to the point of the explosion at Indiana Harbor, had determined that it occurred between certain hours and at a certain point, and that dynamite was used. He then made a thorough investigation to determine whether or not strangers were seen in that vicinity, and also whether it was possible to obtain dynamite there or thereabouts. After covering considerable ground along these lines I finally summed up the result of his investigation, and suggested to him that he was able to return and inform the client positively that the bridge had been dynamited. He admitted that he supposed that about covered the result of his investigation.

He further stated that the McClintic-Marshall Company were running an open shop. They were paying higher wages and the working conditions were better than those required by the Union, but the fight was for the closed shop. I then asked if he was satisfied that the motive was to enforce the closed shop, and that if that were true might it not be possible that the Bridge and Structural Iron Workers' Union was responsible for the explosion. If so, then the proper place for the further investigation would be this Union.

Further inquiry developed the fact that this was one of a great number of similar explosions, amounting to over one hundred, and covering a period of several years.

We then communicated with our clients and asked permission to reopen the Indiana Harbor investigation, but not being impressed with the results thus far obtained, and unquestionably because of the fact that they had paid out tens of thousands of dollars for useless work and with no results, they naturally concluded that it would be of no use to delve further into this. In the meantime, however, I made a personal call on the McClintic-Marshall Company and impressed them with the fact that I would be able to make a successful investigation of that character of work, and was sure I would be able to apprehend those responsible. As a result, when a similar explosion occurred at Peoria, Ill., we were again called in, and this time I took personal charge of the investigation and directed the movements of my operatives.

This was a series of explosions, and did great damage. One charge of ten gallons of nitroglycerin was placed under an 80-ton girder manufactured by McClintic-Marshall, which was intended to span the Illinois River for the Pekin & Peoria R. R. The other took place in the iron works of Lucas & Sons, and both charges exploded at the same hour and the same second, of the same night; the escape of five lives on this occasion was nothing short of miraculous.

It so happened that this night it rained, and for

that reason the railroad watchmen would make a round and then enter a box-car for shelter. They had just entered the car some short distance from the explosion when it occurred. Had they been at any other spot where it was required for them to traverse their work, they would have been killed. At the iron works the watchmen had passed the spot where the explosion took place within only a moment of safety to them.

At the iron works it was learned that J. J. McNamara, the secretary and treasurer of the International Bridge and Structural Iron Workers, and H. S. Hockin, organizer and field worker of the same organization, visited the office only a few days before and strongly urged that the employers run a closed shop. McClintic-Marshall had been notified in advance that the explosion was to take place, and they in turn notified the officers of this concern that there was danger to their property. These officers, notified by the McClintic-Marshall Company, at Peoria and East Peoria, realized that violence might be used by these Structural Iron Workers. Apparently they did not take this advice seriously enough, however, for, on the night of September 4, 1910, at the hour of 10.30, the iron works in East Peoria and the McClintic-Marshall girders in the railroad yards were blown up by nitroglycerin.

CHAPTER III

FOLLOWING A SAWDUST TRAIL

I have always insisted that every criminal leaves a track—that many times Providence interferes to uncover the footprints left by the criminal. And so on this occasion, one charge under a second girder failed to explode, due to the fact that the dry battery used in the clock bomb lost its voltage. In this way we were able to determine the method used by the dynamiters for bringing about those simultaneous explosions, as through this clock-working device they were enabled to set the explosion for 11 hours and 59 minutes and 59 seconds, which would give them plenty of leeway to escape. They could thereby establish a perfect alibi. They figured, of course, on the total destruction of the bomb, which would obliterate every vestige of evidence as to the character of the explosive used.

I detailed the very best operatives in our service to make this investigation and personally directed each step of their operations. They returned several times with final reports, and each time would be sent back to the work to dig further.

Knowing that nitroglycerin could not be transported on railroad trains, we felt that it must have been manufactured within easy reach of where the explosion took place. Besides, the dynamiters used the original can in which they purchased the nitroglycerin. In addition to the can filled with nitroglycerin that failed to explode, there was also an empty can found in the vicinity, and in this same spot were found some grains of sawdust, all of which was carefully gathered up. And this indicates the care with which the trained detective does his work, for, by a similar circumstance many years before, I was able to bring about the conviction of the notorious Bill Brockaway, by finding at the counterfeiting plant an oilcloth apron used by the counterfeiter while printing his notes at 542 Ann Street, West Hoboken, N. J. And at the room of Brockaway on Avenue A, in New York City, I found a small strip of the same oilcloth, with the same peculiar design; and by fitting them together there was the glazed portion missing from the apron that was supplied by the small strip, and vice versa. I was informed by two of the jurymen in the Brockaway case that this bit of important evidence eliminated the last vestige of doubt from their minds, and caused the conviction of Brockaway, who paid the penalty of ten years in prison.

So, by gathering the bits of sawdust found on the same spot, with a can identical to that in which the nitroglycerin was found, it was subsequently proved that it had been left there by the person who purchased the nitroglycerin from Fred Morehart, of Portland, Indiana, who sold it to a man who gave his name as J. W. McGraw. This man's description tallied exactly with that of a man seen in the vicinity, and whom we traced to a hotel at Muncie. We found his signature on the register, and made a tracing of it.

We then determined that all of those dynamitings occurred in the same way, and from that we could deduce the fact that they were guided by the same mind. This deduction having been reached, the next logical step was Indianapolis, which was the headquarters of the International Bridge and Structural Iron Workers' Union. I was convinced that McGraw was working as a dynamiter for the union.

McGraw's excuse in purchasing the nitroglycerin was that he represented the stone quarry of George Clark & Company, and reminded Mr. Morehart of the fact that they had made a former purchase from his concern through a Mr. Kiser. A search was promptly made for Kiser, and he was located in Oklahoma.

One of the essential features which go to make up the efficient detective is the vigilance over small details. Therefore, the operative had in mind the fact that he would follow, step by step, J. W. McGraw, from the time he first met Mr. Morehart, and interrogate Mr. Morehart as to every word spoken.

I assigned an operative to this task. His report shows how he uncovered helpful evidence at this early stage of the investigation.

Operative H. A. G. reports:

"McGraw, at the time he first met Mr. Morehart, stated that he had formerly purchased nitroglycerin from Kiser at Albany, and had gone there on this occasion, August 20, to purchase some more, but was told at Albany that Kiser had gone away, and that Mr. Morehart had the agency at Portland. McGraw then came to Portland and inquired of Mr. O. O. Gaskill, No. 216 Meridian Street, for Morehart. Gaskill says that he never saw McGraw before and merely directed him to Morehart, but did not tell Morehart that he knew McGraw. McGraw told Morehart that he bought some of the stuff of Kiser about June 1, 1906. This was his first purchase from Kiser, but he made other deals later. This Morehart has been unable to verify as Kiser's books and records show no such sales.

"McGraw told Mr. Morehart, on August 20, the date of his first visit, that he represented G. W. Clark & Co., of Peoria, Ill., that they had some very hard rock and they could use nitroglycerin there with better results and less expense than dynamite. He also said that Mr. G. W. Clark lived in Indianapolis. (There is no G. W. Clark in the directories there.) When the stuff was delivered by Morehart to McGraw at Albany on August 30, McGraw had a camera and took a picture of Morehart on his wagon. This is a specially made rig and bears the words in large letters, 'Nitro Glycerine—Dangerous,' on the sides and rear. On it also is the apparatus for well shooting, which business Morehart is engaged in. McGraw gave as a reason for coming to Indiana for the stuff that the roads were much better between there and Peoria and the difference in mileage was more than compensated for on that account. Although McGraw promised Morehart a copy of the picture he took he has never sent it. There were no marks on the boxes which McGraw had on his wagon. The place indicated by me as the spot where the transfer was made and from whence I took the sawdust is pronounced by Morehart as the exact spot where he met McGraw. He remembers very distinctly that the sawdust was unusually coarse stuff. Paper was in the bottom of one of the boxes and was cast aside by McGraw and left lying there when he departed. McGraw was talkative, and was apparently not a drinking man. He proved himself a genuine K. of P., but did not state the name or location of his lodge. He claimed to be well acquainted in Fostoria, Ohio, and mentioned a number of places there with which Morehart is quite familiar. He mentioned no names of acquaintances, however. Fostoria is near Toledo, about 10,000 population, and Morehart is quite sure that if McGraw lived there at any time he could be easily traced in the town. McGraw told Morehart that he had used nitroglycerin, and that he was familiar with its use. In paying Morehart he exhibited a large roll of twenty-dollar bills, and the money he took from the roll did not appreciably diminish its size. McGraw seemed familiar with the proper method of handling the stuff as well as with the law regulating its transportation, storage, etc. He said he would require another consignment in a short time, and would return and obtain it from Morehart. I arranged with Morehart that in case McGraw or any other stranger makes overtures to him for the purchase of any of the stuff in the future, he will put the man off 24 hours on a plea of being out of stock, and he will then communicate by telephone with our Chicago office at once. This he can easily do without arousing suspicion, as it often occurs that the supply is exhausted before a new lot is received."

That little pinch of sawdust taken as a sample near the railroad yards in Peoria came in very handy. It established the fact that the man who bought the nitroglycerin from Morehart had carried some of the explosive and had set it off with the time clock attachment in Peoria. The sample showed that it was the same sawdust as that found sprinkled in the road two hundred miles away at the point where the explosive was transferred from Morehart's vehicle to McGraw's.

We had a good description of McGraw. Next was to get his signature. Operative H. A. G. hunted through the various hotels in the towns around Portland, and finally came to a register in Muncie, Ind., with the name J. W. McGraw upon it. H. A. G. made a tracing of this signature. We then found the liveryman who had rented McGraw a light wagon and the man who had sold him a long-handled shovel observed by Mr. Morehart in the wagon. From these we got good descriptions. My operatives found the sawdust pile in the yard of a farmhouse on the road leading to Morehart's. Here McGraw had stopped to take enough for his needs in packing the explosive. We could now prove that the sawdust found in Peoria was the same sawdust as that stolen from the farmer's yard and the same dropped from the wagon when the nitroglycerin was transferred from Morehart's vehicle to McGraw's. We had made an advance upon the dynamiter that was worth while. We had his description, his signature and a clearly marked trail connecting him from the place where the explosive was bought to where it was touched off. We also had one of his little clock machines. Furthermore we would trap him if he called on Morehart for more nitro.

CHAPTER IV

RICH MAN DRIVEN TO GERMANY

The opening of the trail to McGraw was accomplished after about three weeks of hard work and the running out of many clues that proved valueless. It was the first opening after five years of continued warfare against the employers of structural iron workers by the men who levied on the pay envelopes of those who would work and could get the chance to work; by the men who at International Headquarters in Indianapolis used this money for their own ends, for drink and the payment of money to blackmailing women; by the men who never did a day's honest work themselves and whose only occupation outside of licentious indulgence was the occupation of destruction and murder.

It was indeed a reign of terror. The police are always in politics, and politics in the police system. The labor leaders are in politics, and this triangular state of affairs made it no cause for wonder that no one was arrested and no crime was avenged by the law.

If the United States was a free country during those five years the employers did not have good

reason to believe it. A record of over one hundred
cases of assault on non-union workers during that
time is available. It ranges from throwing acid in
the face of a worker to the hurling of a special po-
liceman from the structure of the Hotel Plaza in
New York City when that building was in course of
erection. The officer was slugged first and then
thrown to his death to hide the marks of the assault.

David M. Parry, formerly president of the National Association of Manufacturers, a wealthy resident of Indianapolis, incurred the hatred of the
leaders of the hidden forces. He was compelled to
walk about the streets of his native city with a
heavy bodyguard and with an automatic revolver
in each coat pocket. Mr. Parry is a dead shot,
and is afraid of no man. His brother is the cham-
pion pistol shot of the National Guards of Indiana.
It sounds like melodrama, but the two Parrys were
ready to make somebody pay for their taking off.
The telephone was kept busy in Mr. D. M. Parry's
office by people who made threats to kill him and
burn his house. He surrounded his splendid residence with guards and kept on his course.

Finally the terrorists threatened to kidnap his
children. The father's heart in Mr. Parry beat
with fear at this threat. He determined to move
his family abroad, and he took his wife and children
to Strasburg in Germany. There he got a home for
them until the reign of terror would come to an end.

He, a millionaire 'American citizen, then went to the chief of police of this German city and recited the facts and asked that should his enemies pursue his family to Strasburg police protection be given them.

All the while the planted mines and bombs were being set off. Here is a partial list of explosions from the time of the declaration of the strike of the structural workers up to the terrible climax of the first of October, 1910, when the Los Angeles Times Building was utterly destroyed with twenty-one innocent people:

No.	Date.	Location.	Contractor.	Owner.	Nature of work.	Nature and extent of damage.
1	Summer, 1905	New Haven, Conn., Kimberly Avenue.	American Bridge Co.	City of New Haven and town of Orange.	Bridge over West River.	Dynamite discovered in fire box of hoisting engine.
2	Dec. 8, 1905	Millers Falls, Mass.	...do...	Central Vermont R. R.	Railroad bridge	13 sticks of dynamite discovered; fuse had been lighted, but became extinguished before fire reached dynamite.
3	Mar. 12, 1906	Cleveland, Ohio, Hotel Frankfort.	...do...			Attempt made to dynamite hotel occupied by nonunion workmen in employ of the American Bridge Co.
4	Apr. 2, 1906	Cleveland, Ohio.	...do...		Arcade Building	3 sticks of dynamite discovered in fire box of hoisting engine, with fuse attached, which had been lighted.
5	May 12, 1906		...do...	Buffalo & Susquehanna R. R.	Railroad bridge.	Attempt made to dynamite derrick car.
6	May 31, 1906	Newark, N. J.	Pittsburgh Construction Co.	Central R. R. of New Jersey.	Warehouse.	Derrick in storage yard wrecked by dynamite.
7	Aug. 15, 1906	Conshohocken, Pa.	McClintic-Marshall Construction Co.	Longmead Iron Co.	Iron Mill.	Damaged to extent of several thousand dollars by incendiary fire.
8	Sept. 25, 1906	Cleveland, Ohio.	Pittsburgh Construction Co.	Nickel Plate R. R.	Railroad viaduct.	Attempt made to dynamite derrick car; explosive (with time clock and fuse) evidently thrown from passing train.
9	Oct. 12, 1906	Near Clairton, Pa.	American Bridge Co.	Pittsburgh, Virginia & Charleston Ry.; West Side Belt Line Ry.	Viaduct.	Derrick car dynamited.
10	Dec. 30, 1906, 8.30 p. m.	Whisky Island, near Cleveland, Ohio.	Pittsburgh Construction		Bascule bridge over Cuyahoga River.	Dynamite placed under derrick car; damage slight.
11	June 25, 1907, about 1 a. m.	Detroit, Mich.	Russel Wheel & Foundry Co.	Detroit City Gas Co.	Detroit City Gas Co. building.	Building dynamited during erection of steelwork; buildings in vicinity also damaged.
12	September, 1907	Cleveland, Ohio.	American Bridge Co.	American Steel & Wire Co.	American Steel & Wire Co. plant.	Hoisting engine totally destroyed by dynamite.
13	Oct. 30, 1907	Youngstown, Ohio.	Youngstown Construction Co.	Baltimore & Ohio R. R.	Railroad bridge.	Bridge slightly damaged by explosion.
14	Dec. 23, 1907	Near Harrison, N. J.	Brann & Stuart Co.	Pennsylvania R. R.	Railroad bridge over Newark branch of Erie R. R.	Girder and floor of bridge damaged by explosion; about $2,000 damage.
15	Dec. 31, 1907, between 7 and 8 p. m.	Cleveland, Ohio (?) Parma Road.	Lucius Co.	Cleveland Short Line R. R.	Bridge.	Two tons of material damaged so they had to be replaced; loss $500.

No.	Date.	Location.	Contractor.	Owner.	Nature of work.	Nature and extent of damage.
16	Dec. 31, 1907, between 7 and 8. p. m.	Mill Creek	Lucius	Lake Erie & Pittsburgh Ry.	Viaduct	Ten tons of material damaged so they had to be replaced; loss, $1,200.
17	Jan. 17, 1908	Cleveland, Ohio, Eagle Avenue.	Interstate Engineering Co.	Big Four R. R. (?)	Bridge	Girders for above bridge in railroad yards damaged by dynamite; car and surrounding property also damaged.
18	Jan. 31, 1908	Elsdon, Ill	McClintic-Marshall Construction Co.		Building	One column damaged by explosion of dynamite and couple of girts bent; damage, $150.
19	Feb. 3, 1908, about 10.30 p. m.	Pelham, N. Y	American Bridge Co	City of New York	Scherzer Drawbridge over Eastchester Bay.	Guy clamps on 4 guys which were used to hold the draw were removed, causing draw to roll forward and fall into the bay; damage between $5,000 and $10,000.
20	Feb. 17, 1908	Clinton, Iowa	Wisconsin Bridge & Iron Co.	Chicago & Northwestern Ry. Co.	Double-track bridge over Mississippi River.	30 sticks of dynamite placed in various parts of derrick car; 1 lot exploded, rest being frozen; damage, about $2,000.
21	Mar. 18, 1908	Chicago, Ill, Buena Park	Pittsburgh Construction Co.	Chicago, Milwaukee & St. Paul R. R.		Derrick car and surrounding property considerably damaged by dynamite.
22	Mar. 25, 1908, a. m.	Perth Amboy, N. J	Pennsylvania Steel Co		Drawbridge over Raritan River.	Bridge damaged by dynamite to extent of about $1,500.
23	Mar. 25, 1908, about 12.15 a. m.	Near Bradshaw, Md.	Youngstown Construction Co.	Baltimore & Ohio R. R.	Railroad bridge.	Traveler used in erection of this work partially destroyed by dynamite.
24	Apr. 1, 1908	New York City, N. Y.	Pennsylvania Steel Co.	City of New York	Blackwells Island Bridge.	Wire falls rigged up for anchorage of 10-ton derrick, on top of temporary tower for removing temporary traveler were loosened, but discovered in time to prevent accident.
25	Apr. 2, 1908, a. m.	do	do	do	do	Manila boom-fall line for 10-ton derrick on top of traveler cut; derrick was not being operated.
26	Apr. 5, 1908, p. m.	New York City, N. Y., Chelsea Piers.	McClintic-Marshall Construction Co.	do	Pier 58, North River	Hoisting crane damaged by dynamite and engine demolished; damage, from $500 to $1,000.
27	Apr. 9, 1908, p. m.	Near West Farms Station, N. Y.	Lewis F. Shoemaker & Co.		Highway Bridge, Tremont Avenue.	Guy clamps on wire guys on 60-ton derrick removed causing mast of derrick to topple over; depredation discovered just in time to prevent accident to passenger train.

No.	Date.	Location.	Contractor.	Owner.	Nature of work.	Nature and extent of damage.
28	Apr. 13, 1908, about 11 p. m.	Philadelphia, Pa., Federal Yard of Pennsylvania R. R.	American Bridge Co.	Delaware Avenue Elevated R. R.	Elevated road	Material for job damaged by two charges of dynamite to extent of about $1,000.
29	Apr. 26, 1908, a. m.	Fall River, Mass.	....do....	Bristol County, Mass.	Slades Ferry Bridge over Taunton River.	Two spans damaged by dynamite; loss, between $2,000 and $3,000.
30	May 3, 1908 (Sunday), about 12 p. m.	Dayton, Ohio.	....do....	Cincinnati, Hamilton & Dayton Ry.	Railway bridge over Miami River.	Derrick car damaged by dynamite.
31	May 21, 1908, p. m.	New York, N. Y.	Pennsylvania Steel Co.	New York, New Haven & Hartford R. R.	Scherzer Drawbridge over Bronx River.	Attempt made to dynamite bridge; suitcase found in river contained 103 sticks of dynamite and 2 coils of fuse.
32	May 22, 1908, a. m.	Baychester, N. Y.	Lewis F. Shoemaker & Co.	....do....	Highway bridge.	Bridge damaged by dynamite to extent of about $1,500.
33	May 24, 1908, 1.30 a. m.	Aiken, Md.	Youngstown Construction Co.	Baltimore & Ohio R. R.	Bridge.	Attempt made to dynamite job; 5 sticks of dynamite found—dropped by man seen running away from job.
34	June 2, 1908, a. m.	Perryville, Md.	American Bridge Co.	....do....	Railroad bridge over Susquehanna River.	Attempt made to dynamite job by 4 men who ran away, leaving dynamite behind.
35	June 2, 1908, p. m.	Cleveland, Ohio.		Van Dorn Iron Wks. Co.	Plant of Van Dorn Iron Works Co.	20-ton steel derrick wrecked, wall of steel building twisted out of shape and part of railroad siding torn out by dynamite; loss, $500; 14 unexploded sticks of dynamite found, attached to partly burned fuse.
36	June 15, 1908, 10.30 p. m.	Somerset, Mass.	Phoenix Bridge Co.	New York, New Haven & Hartford R. R.	Taunton River Bridge.	Material for above bridge, in storage yard, dynamited; damage, about $1,000.
37	July 1, 1908, about 2.45 a. m.	Buffalo, N. Y.	McClintic-Marshall Construction Co.	Lehigh Valley R. R.	Railroad bridge.	Girders damaged to extent of about $1,500 by two charges of dynamite; explosion occurred a few minutes prior to arrival of passenger train, which was stopped at end of bridge within 200 feet of where explosion occurred.
38	Aug. 6, 1908, p. m.	Chicago, Ill., Onehundred and thirty-third Street.	American Bridge Co.	Illinois Central R. R.	Railroad bridge over Calumet River.	Bridge damaged by dynamite explosion.
39	Aug. 6, 1908.	Cincinnati, Ohio.	Grainger Construction Co.		Harrison Avenue Viaduct.	Viaduct damaged by either dynamite or nitroglycerin.

No.	Date.	Location.	Contractor.	Owner.	Nature of work.	Nature and extent of damage.
40	Aug. 9, 1908, 2 a. m.	St. Louis, Mo.	....	....	Eighteenth Street bridge, being repaired.	Two charges of dynamite exploded on bridge, which was being repaired by nonunion men.
41	Oct. 15, 1908.	Holyoke, Mass.	Lewis F. Shoemaker & Co.	New York, New Haven & Hartford R. R.	Plate girder bridge.	Attempt made to dynamite bridge; watchman discovered burning fuse, and put it out.
42	Nov. 30, 1908, 7.05 p. m.	Cleveland, Ohio.	Pittsburgh Construction Co.	Wheeling & Lake Erie R. R.	Railroad bridge.	Concrete pedestal and column wrecked by dynamite; damage, about $500.
43	Mar. 18, 1909.	Indiana Harbor, Ind.	...do...	Erie R. R.	....	Car of steel dynamited near job; damage about $100.
44	Mar. 24, 1909, about 1 a. m.	...do...	...do...	....	....	Two packages of dynamite, with fuse attached, were thrown from a Lake Shore freight train, passing work of above company; no damage.
45	Mar. 27, 1909.	Boston, Mass.	Geo. W. Harvey Co.	....	New Opera House.	Southeast side of building destroyed by dynamite; being erected by nonunion men.
46	Mar. 31, 1909, about 3 a. m.	Hoboken, N. J.	McClintic-Marshall Construction Co.	City of Hoboken.	Viaduct.	Columns and other parts of bridge wrecked by dynamite; also several buildings nearby; 5 or 6 people injured; damage, $1,000.
47	Apr. 29, 1909.	Kansas City, Mo.	A. M. Blodgett Construction Co.	....	....	Derrick car dynamited; damage slight.
48	May 9, 1909.	Cincinnati, Ohio.	Pittsburgh Construction Co.	Cincinnati Southern R. R.	Railroad bridge.	Charge of dynamite exploded; damage slight.
49	May 24, 1909, 8.15 p. m. Monday.	...do...	...do...	...do...	...do...	Two charges of dynamite placed on top of pier on which girders were resting; damage, $300.
50	June 7, 1909.	Buffalo, N. Y., East Ferry Street.	....	New York Central & Hudson River R. R.	Railroad bridge, completed.	Bridge dynamited; several thousand dollars damage done. It is thought that a bridge being erected by the McCain Construction Co. (who did not employ union labor exclusively) was the one intended to be dynamited.
51	June 26, 1909.	Steubenville, Ohio.	Seaboard Construction Co.	Pennsylvania R. R.	Bridge.	Material for bridge, on cars, dynamited; estimated damage, $2,500.
52	...do...	Kansas City, Mo., Main Street.	A. M. Blodgett Construction Co.	....	Viaduct.	One pier dynamited; loss, about $75.

No.	Date.	Location.	Contractor.	Owner.	Nature of work.	Nature and extent of damage.
53	July 9, 1909..........	Detroit, Mich., Beecher Avenue.	....	Whitehead & Kales.	Plant of company..	Suitcase containing guncotton placed under pile of steel girders in yard of plant; explosion destroyed girders and did considerable damage to nearby factories, etc.
54	Aug. 12, 1909, about 12 m.	Cincinnati, Ohio........	Pittsburgh Construction Co.	Cincinnati Southern Ry.	Viaduct..........	Two girders in street along route of viaduct damaged by dynamite; damage, $600 to $700.
55	Aug. 16, 1909, 12.05 a. m.	Bronx, New York City, One hundred and fifty-sixth Street.	...do....	New York, New Haven & Hartford R. R.	Railroad bridge No. 211.	Two angles bent by explosion of dynamite; damage about $20.
56	Sept. 5, 1909, p. m......	Hoboken, N. J., Fourteenth Street.	McClintic-Marshall Construction Co.	City of Hoboken...	Viaduct..........	15 sticks of dynamite and fuse discovered after 4 men were frightened away from the job.
57	Sept. 14, 1909, p. m.....	Buffalo, N. Y., near corner of Elk and Michigan Streets.	McCain Construction Co.	....	Viaduct over New York Central & Hudson River R. R. tracks.	Derrick car and track destroyed by dynamite. (See explosion of June 7, 1909.)
58	Oct. 6, 1909..........	Buffalo N. Y., near corner of Elk and Michigan Streets.	...do....	....	Viaduct over New York Central & Hudson River R. R. tracks.	One column damaged by dynamite; also adjoining property and windows within block.
59	Oct. 25, 1909, a. m......	Indianapolis, Ind......	Albert Von Spreckelsen.	....	Central Union Exchange Building; public library building; Von Spreckelsen planing mill; Von Spreckelsen barn.	Above buildings all dynamited at practically the same time; total damage about $15,000. Dynamitings followed employment of non-union men.
60	Nov. 4, 1909, p. m......	Cleveland, Ohio, Cuyahoga River.	Brown Hoisting & Machinery Co.	Corrigan-McKinney Co.	Crane..........	Crane, freight cars, tracks and foundations in neighborhood wrecked by dynamite. Watchman narrowly escaped death; damage, $40,000.
61	Nov. 21, 1909, Sunday.	Green Bay, Wis........	Wisconsin Bridge & Iron Co.	....	....	Car of steel dynamited.
62	Dec. 29, 1909, Wednesday, about 3.35 a. m.	Salt Lake City, Utah..	R. D. Jones, subcontractor for Amer. Bridge Co.	....	Utah Hotel........	Two heavy charges of dynamite exploded in building.
63	Mar. 27, 1910, Sunday, 9.30 p. m.	Indiana Harbor, Ind....	McClintic-Marshall Construction Co.	American Steel Foundries Co.	American Steel Foundries Co. plant.	Two columns and bases destroyed by bombs with time fuses attached; damage about $500.

No.	Date.	Location.	Contractor.	Owner.	Nature of work.	Nature and extent of damage.
64	Apr. 5, 1910.	New Castle, Ind.		Pan-American Bridge Co.	Plant of Pan-American Bridge Co.	Plant dynamited.
65	Apr. 18, 1910, a. m.	Salt Lake City, Utah.	R. D. Jones, subcontractor for American Bridge Co.		Utah Hotel.	Dynamite exploded under framework of hotel; steelwork only slightly damaged.
66	Apr. 19, 1910.	Clinton, Ind.		Chicago & Eastern Illinois R. R.	Railroad bridge over Wabash River.	Two explosions of dynamite wrecked 2 piers of bridge and shattered stonework and iron braces to such an extent that traffic was abandoned.
67	Apr. 19, 1910, 11.30 p. m.	Mount Vernon, Ill.	McClintic-Marshall Construction Co.	Mount Vernon Car & Manufacturing Co.	Power house.	Hoisting engine completely destroyed by explosion; locomotive crane also damaged.
68	May 24, 1910, 1 a. m.	New York City, Two hundred and twenty-third Street, near Broadway.	Pennsylvania Steel Co.		Viaduct.	Material stored on dock damaged by dynamite; loss between $700 and $800. After the explosion parts of an alarm clock, leather suitcase, and dry battery were found.
69	June 4, 1910, 3.30 a. m.	Davenport, Iowa.	McClintic-Marshall Construction Co.	Davenport Locomotive Works.	Machine shop.	Two columns damaged by explosion.
70	June 4, 1910, 12 p. m.	Peoria, Ill.	....do....	Peoria & Pekin Union Ry.	Bridge.	Two girders damaged by dynamite.
71	June 22, 1910, 2 a. m.	Cleveland, Ohio.	....do....	Cuyahoga County.	Denison-Harvard Viaduct.	Several trusses to be used in above viaduct wrecked by dynamite; loss,$100.
72	July 4, 1910.	Akron, Ohio.	The Burger Iron Co.	Diamond Rubber Co.	Building.	Dynamite explosion; damage slight.
73	July 9, 1910, 2.45 and 3.20 a. m.	Jersey City, N.J. (Greenville), foot of Bidwell Avenue.	Phoenix Bridge Co.	Lehigh Valley R. R.	Viaduct.	2 explosions wrecked 2 legs of water supporting viaduct; about $1,000 damage.
74	July 15, 1910, 2 a. m.	Pittsburgh, Pa., West (McCarson Street Kees Rocks).	McClintic-Marshall Construction Co.	West Wide Belt R. R.	Trestlework.	2 concrete piers and floor beam shattered by dynamite; damage, about $800.
75	July 21, 1910, about 12 p. m.	Omaha, Nebr.	Wisconsin Bridge & Iron Co.	Omaha & Council Bluffs Street Ry.	Power plant.	2 beams destroyed by explosion; some steel bent; damage between $125 and $150.
76	Aug. 1, 1910, 12 p. m.; Aug. 2, 1910, 12.30 a. m.	Superior, Wis.	Heyl & Patterson.	Philadelphia & Reading Coal & Iron Co.	Unloading rig on new Connors Point Dock.	Truck destroyed by explosion.
77	Aug. 20, 1910.	Oakland, Cal.		Pacific Coast Lumber Co.	Mill of Pacific Coast Lumber Co.	Wrecked by exploding dynamite. (Fourth time in last 2 years this mill has been wrecked.)

No.	Date.	Location.	Contractor.	Owner.	Nature of work.	Nature and extent of damage.
78	Aug. 23, 1910, 8.30 p. m.	Kansas City, Mo.	McClintic-Marshall Construction Co.		Railroad bridge	Material in yards at foot of Holmes Street dynamited; damage, about $200.
79	Aug. 31, 1910	Seattle, Wash.			Office building	Wrecked by dynamite.
80	Sept. 4, 1910	Peoria, Ill.		Lucas Bridge & Iron Co.	Plant	3 explosions of dynamite; plant badly damaged; also 6 adjacent buildings; night watchman seriously injured.
81	do.	East Peoria, Ill.	McClintic-Marshall Construction Co.	Peoria & Pekin Union Ry.	Railroad bridge	2 carloads of steel girders to be used in construction of bridge, dynamited; only 2 girders damaged.
82	Sept. 15, 1910, about 10 p. m.	Chicago, Ill.	Winslow Bros	Winslow Bros, plant		Woodwork, windows and masonry completely shattered by explosion of bomb with time fuse placed in entrance to building. Had explosion occurred few minutes later, night watchman would have been killed. (Explosion followed visit of delegation from Chicago Federation of Labor.)
83	Sept. 27, 1910, about 1 a. m.	Nicetown, Pa.	American Bridge Co.	Philadelphia & Reading Ry.	Grade crossing bridges	Traveler dynamited; little damage done.

39

CHAPTER V

ATTEMPT TO KILL PRESIDENT TAFT

The explosions given in the preceding chapter all occurred prior to October 1, 1910, the date of the Los Angeles Times destruction. They did not stop then by any means. In fact, the terrorists were not satisfied even with this terrible climax of the five years' war. They sent back to Los Angeles a man with nitroglycerin and dynamite to destroy the auxiliary plant of the newspaper and the Baker and Llewellyn Iron Works. And then to give the idea that these crimes were locally conducted affairs they set off two bombs in Worcester, Mass., on October 10. There were twenty-five explosions altogether in the year 1910, and they went on during the first part of the year 1911, amounting to ten in number, until the arrest of the McNamaras, which was on April 12.

There were no explosions or attempts to dynamite after the arrests. But in October of 1911 an attempt was made to blow up a Southern Pacific Railroad bridge near Santa Barbara, Cal., just before a train bearing the President of the United States was due to cross it. Thirty-nine sticks of dynamite with fuse attached were found in the bridge structure by a watchman.

A careful estimate shows that to perpetrate all of these crimes between three and four hundred quarts of nitroglycerin and over 2,000 pounds of dynamite were lugged about the country in passenger trains to the imminent peril of thousands of innocent men, women and children. A heavy jolt in coupling, a slight accident and a train would have been blown to pieces on the rails.

It is almost impossible to conceive that human beings in a stage of civilization could have so lightly borne responsibility for the preservation of their own kind. Things were done in the bloody war culminating in the Los Angeles disaster that would not be tolerated on fields of battle in the Far East. One railroad bridge that had been built by non-union men was destroyed by the wreckers employed by the McNamaras just before a heavily loaded passenger train reached it. Another minute and every man, woman and child on that train would have been sent to death.

The cost of this warfare for both sides was tremendous. The actual cost in material and structures damaged or destroyed for one hundred explosions was figured at more than a million. The loss to the companies aside from this ran higher, for every job and every plant had to be heavily picketed with guards. On one job alone in Cleveland a company paid $17,000 for guards. Then, too, is the loss from contracts unfulfilled or delayed, the cutting down of the degree of efficiency as the result of fear following these attacks and employees giving up their work through intimidation.

The McNamaras were given and spent one thousand dollars a month for two and a half years to finance the murder and destruction. That money came out of the pockets of the comparatively few men of the union who held jobs and from contributions made by other unions. The working union man was gouged for at least $190,000 for the defense of the two McNamaras, who didn't work, but who spent the money of those who did work on drink, on women and for nitroglycerin and the hire of Anarchists. The trial in Indianapolis, where forty-five union "leaders" answered the charge of conspiracy, cost the working union man $5,000 a week. The trial lasted three months or more.

What it cost in lost wages to the men who were ordered on strike and kept on strike during this period of warfare it is almost impossible to conjecture. Days, weeks, months and years of living from hand to mouth, of character being sapped by hanging about corner saloons, of homes partly paid for being sacrificed, of women and children half starved and half clothed, of drunkenness, despair and poverty. The price was frightful. Moreover, the union, built up, after years of struggle, into a large organization, was ruined. The cause of organized labor was pushed back a quarter of a century.

Wealth did not do this, the laws of the country did not do it. Anarchy did it.

Ending this digression, we will go back to the first day of October, 1910, when newspapers the world over told the story of the destruction of the Los Angeles Times and all the people at work in the building.

CHAPTER VI

BURNS BUSY IN LOS ANGELES

On the first day of October, 1910, I was on my way to the Pacific Coast to attend the convention of the American Bankers' Association, my agency being under contract to guard the banks of the Association from thieves and yeggmen.

I was en route when I received word from Mayor George B. Alexander of Los Angeles asking me to take up the investigation of the destruction of the Times.

Los Angeles seemed to be in a state of panic. Another earthquake would not have created such fear as the citizens were experiencing. An earthquake is an act of nature, but what was going on in Los Angeles was the act of a cunning, heartless, ruthless enemy of society. It seemed as if a homicidal maniac of the most terrible type was doing his work. The shattered walls of the Times building were still sending a column of smoke to the sky and beneath the wreckage lay twenty-one human beings, broken, dead and charred. Crowding the police lines were the wives and children of these innocent victims of the masked war. The white faces of these widows and children were strained with horror, and their cries of anguish broke above the excited talk of the crowd.

A great quantity of eighty per cent gelatin—dynamite—had been exploded in an interior alley of the building among the rolls of paper and barrels of ink stored there. Eighty per cent gelatin is of such tremendous explosive power that it is seldom made or sold. It is the kind of stuff that might be used in blowing up the fortress of an enemy in time of open and fair war. The destruction it had wrought was complete and awful.

But this work, as terrible as it was, did not seem to have been sufficient to appease the craving of the men who lurked in the dark. They had also placed under the home of General Harrison Gray Otis, the proprietor of the Times, enough explosive to wreck it and kill his family. So also had they placed an infernal machine under the home of the secretary of the Merchants and Manufacturers' Association. Both of these mines were set to spring at the time the newspaper building was destroyed. Had the plan worked out, Los Angeles would have been shaken from one end to the other, and two homes would have gone to destruction with all in them, as the Times building was destroyed.

The bomb under the home of General Otis was discovered in time. A detective cut open the suit case in which it was hidden, but the time clock within had ticked off the moment for the explosion. He heard the whirr of the alarm winder and ran. The bomb exploded in the open and no damage was done. The other bomb failed to explode, the battery being so weak that it proved ineffective.

The Mayor called on me at the Hotel Alexandria and there urged me to take up the investigation. I assured him that I would, and at the same time informed him that we were already investigating the work of the same dynamiters, and that I was sure I would be able to apprehend those responsible for the explosion at Los Angeles. Not only that, I gave the Mayor the names of the men responsible for the blowing up of the Los Angeles Times. This did not impress the Mayor, however, as he merely looked upon this as the proverbial speculation of the detective. Subsequently, however, as told by the Mayor himself, when we apprehended those responsible for it, he then realized, for the first time, the great importance of my first statement, which accurately outlined, in a speculative way, those who were later found to be actually guilty.

I cautioned the Mayor, on this occasion, that if I was to make the investigation that fact should be confined to as few people as possible, and my connection with the investigation should be kept an absolute secret. He agreed with me, and left. Within an hour he returned and stated that a most peculiar situation existed in Los Angeles. The town was divided into two political factions.

In view of the fact that I had made the graft investigation at San Francisco, and had sought to jail those responsible for the frightful municipal conditions found there, and because of the further fact that I was no respecter of persons, but had sought to do my whole duty and place the responsibility upon the shoulders of the men who were responsible for the debauchery of San Francisco, I had incurred the ill will of those involved, together with their friends. General Otis, the owner of the Times, believing that the street-car strike in San Francisco was really genuine and brought about by an honest vote of the employees of the Street Railway Company, sympathized, naturally, with the owners of the company, and his paper was fighting for what he considered *industrial freedom* and the *"open" shop,* and therefore believed the falsehoods that were circulated by the Calhoun element. Naturally, he opposed my selection to make this investigation, as he had been bitterly denouncing me in his newspaper.

The Mayor notified me that this element, represented by General Otis and the Merchants & Manufacturers' Association of Los Angeles, insisted that they be represented by a Los Angeles lawyer named Rodgers, who was one of the Calhoun attorneys at San Francisco. The Mayor strongly objected to the selection of Rodgers, and informed the representatives of the Merchants & Manufacturers' Association, and also the Citizens' Committee, which he had appointed, that he was sure I would not care to coöperate with Rodgers. They insisted, however, and urged the Mayor to call on me again, which he did. When he apprised me of what the situation was, I promptly told him to turn the entire matter over to the Merchants & Manufacturers' Association and the Citizens' Committee, as I would certainly not coöperate with Rodgers; that he was a lawyer and not a detective, and what they needed at that time was the service of the latter. The Mayor then returned to the conference, and so notified those interested. A scramble ensued, in which it was charged that the Mayor did not want to apprehend those responsible for the blowing up of the Times, and that he had purposely urged me not to accept.

When he returned to me and stated these facts he pointed out that he was placed in rather a peculiar situation, and that unless I would consent to act with Rodgers, he, the Mayor, would always be blamed if they failed to apprehend the dynamiters, and that this failure would be used, as the Mayor explained, to discredit his administration. The Mayor was visibly affected by this charge, and I promptly assured him that I would agree to coöperate with Rodgers in case a conference in which I was to participate should fail to eliminate Rodgers. We then repaired to the office of the Chief of Police, where the conference was taking place. I pointed out the fact that it was not necessary to have Mr. Rodgers in the matter. But one of the reasons advocated by a member of the conference as to the necessity of having Rodgers was the fact that Rodgers was able to determine when we had proper evidence. I assured them that I was as able, if not more so, to determine that fact as was Mr. Rodgers. However, the upshot of it all was that Mr. Rodgers was brought in, and we "buried the hatchet." Rodgers and myself then held a conference, in which I outlined the preliminary steps to be taken, especially the fact that it should all be done in the strictest secrecy possible, and not exploited in the newspapers, and that I should not be known in the investigation at all. This was perfectly agreeable to Mr. Rodgers.

I then wired my Chicago office to dispatch, as quickly as possible, two of the operatives who participated in the Peoria investigation, and to bring with them the unexploded bomb found at Peoria. When they arrived, and we compared the unexploded bomb that was found at the residence of the secretary, with the unexploded bomb that was found at Los Angeles at the home of the Secretary of the Merchants and Manufacturers' Association, it was disclosed that both were fashioned by the same hand, which left no doubt whatever as to the identity of the persons responsible.

CHAPTER VII

TRACING UNEXPLODED BOMB

I turned over to my operatives the unexploded bomb found by the police in Los Angeles and put them to work tracing it to its maker. One of the reports of "H. A. G." tells of their work.

H. A. G. reports:

"Accompanied by Assistant Manager C. J. S., I called this morning on Principal W. J. B., and, by appointment, met Mayor Alexander and Chief of Police Galloway. The latter gentleman produced the apparatus used by the men who left an infernal machine found unexploded at the residence of the secretary of the Merchants & Manufacturers' Association. It consisted of a small intermittent alarm clock, made by the New Haven Clock Company, and a No. 5 Columbia dry battery. These two mentioned articles were fastened by wire to a small board. On the clock, soldered to the alarm key, is a small piece of brass. A similar brass plate is fastened by a screw and nut to the board—the two pieces of brass forming the contact for exploding the dynamite by means of wires attached from clock to battery.

"This apparatus is identically the same as that which was found in East Peoria, Illinois, on September 5, 1910. The manner in which the brass plate is grooved to fit the winding key, the similarity of the soldering job, which shows skill, the kind of brass and screw used, the manner of fastening the articles to the board, and the fact that the battery and clock are of the same manufacture, as those found in Peoria, would seem to indicate the same person placing them here who placed them in Peoria.

"The stamped letters on the bottom of the battery are rather indistinct, but a capital 'L' is distinguishable. The letters on the battery found at Peoria are 'O 24 Y.'

"His Honor, the Mayor, and Chief of Police Galloway were informed that we have been fortunate enough in the East to prevent any account of our investigations being published and that it was highly important that similar conditions should obtain here and the reporters be prevented from obtaining any information as to the movements made or evidence collected by this Agency.

"A further comparison may be derived from the following brief account of the explosions in Indianapolis, Indiana, and Peoria, Illinois:

"At Indianapolis, on October 25, 1909, at one o'clock a. m., three different structures in the course of erection, under the direction of Contractor Von Spreckelsen, and situated at remote parts of the city from each other, were partially destroyed by explosions which were set off at exactly the same moment. At the same time Von Spreckelsen's barn was burned, destroying two automobiles. The fire occurred simultaneously with the three explosions.

"Three men are known to have been implicated and several others suspected. An automobile was used in this instance and three men used it to leave the city immediately after the affair. It was a gray machine. A similar auto was used in connection with the Peoria affair.

"At 10.30 p. m. on the night of September 4, 1910, two large girders in East Peoria belonging to the McClintic-Marshall Construction Company, and intended for a new railroad bridge across the Illinois River, were destroyed, and at the same instant the works of Lucas & Sons, at Peoria, about three miles distant, were almost totally wrecked by two explosions occurring in their plant.

"On the following day searchers discovered, in East Peoria, a can containing ten quarts of nitroglycerin leaning against one of the girders within a few feet of those destroyed. Inserted in the can were two wires, terminating in a large fulminating cap, such as is used for the purpose of firing explosives; the other ends of the wires being attached to a battery and clock. The battery was a Columbia dry battery, No. 5, and the clock was an intermittent alarm clock, made by the New Haven Clock Company. These were wired to a small board upon

which was bolted a piece of brass and a similar strip
of the same material was soldered to the winding
key of the clock in such a manner that when the
alarm was released the two pieces of brass would
form a contact and explode the cap by means of
the battery. This apparatus was identically the
same as that now in possession of the Los Angeles
authorities."

We began that very day to trace the battery
found in Los Angeles, and found the man who had
sold it and others to the dynamiter. We got a good
description of the man and we learned that few of
this particular make of battery were sold. The
one in question had corroded and had become so
weak that it had failed to set off the explosive.

CHAPTER VIII

BURNS HIMSELF SHADOWED

I had good reason to believe that San Francisco would afford me the field most productive of material upon which to bend my efforts and I proceeded there immediately. I was somewhat hampered with the endeavors of the Los Angeles local investigators, but managed to keep in the background while the newspaper men followed them and were given interviews.

It was through Captain Peterson, of the Oakland Police Department—now the chief of the force there—that I gained much aid in unraveling the mystery of who blew up the Los Angeles Times. It was through him that I got a glimpse of the boat used by the dynamiters in carrying their cargo of explosives to Los Angeles. Chief of Police Seymour of San Francisco, one of the ablest men in police craft, also aided me a great deal while I was investigating there the source of supply of the dynamiters and their method of transporting it.

I learned without difficulty the source of the supply. The very analysis of the dynamite that did not explode in Los Angeles would give me this information. I was near the place of manufactory and knew just how the stuff was taken to Los Angeles. I was getting nearer to the heels of the men who had done this frightful crime and yet, all the time, I was myself being shadowed by detectives evidently employed by two inimical forces: one force representing the people who opposed me in the San Francisco exposures and the other force, the people who had caused the blowing up of the Times in Los Angeles. I knew that I was shadowed all the time. I could not help but know it. After I had finished that part of the investigation necessary for trailing the men who had bought the dynamite and transported it to Los Angeles and was ready to start from San Francisco to my next point, I was compelled to send my baggage out of the city by one way and then take a train by a circuitous route, with my operative, Mr. H. A. Greaves, in order to shake these followers from my heels.

But before ridding myself of this annoyance I had been able to get material evidence in San Francisco and the neighborhood of the city.

I found that the dynamite used in Los Angeles had been made by the Giant Powder Company, and that Mr. Bruce McCall, one of the salesmen for the firm, had attended to the details of the sale. Two men, giving the names of Morris and Bryson, had bought the explosive through him. I looked up Mr. McCall and also Manager R. H. Rennie of the sales department and Thomas J. Branson, the secretary of the company.

Mr. McCall said that about two o'clock on September 15, he received a call on the telephone from a man who said that he represented the Bryce Construction Company of Sacramento. The man on the phone said that he wanted some eighty per cent. gelatin and that he would send for it the next day.

On Friday, September 16, at about 2.30 p. m., a man called at the office of the Giant Powder Company, and gave the name of Bryson. When Mr. McCall reminded him that the name given over the telephone was Bryce, he corrected McCall, and claimed that the name had been given as Bryson. This man said, when asked for what purpose he desired such high power dynamite, that he needed it to blow stumps at a place near Auburn, Cal., as they were very hard to get out and that he had broken several stump pullers trying to get them out. Mr. McCall stated that this strength of gelatin was too strong and more expensive than necessary. Bryson insisted on getting it, stating that he had a contract with a man named Clarke who was doing the work and that the contract specified the 80 per cent. gelatin. He was told that they had none of the 80 per cent. on hand, and he then asked for 90 per cent., and was told that that also was not in stock. He then again insisted on having 80 per cent. gelatin, and was informed that they would have it made up and that he would then be able to get it. He paid Mr. McCall the sum of eighty-two dollars and ten cents ($82.10), eighty dollars of currency in twenty-dollar bills and $2.10 in silver. The bills were United States gold certificates.

This man had quite a large amount of currency, which he took from the inside pocket of his coat in a flat package, taking them from a book of some kind. He was apparently an Eastern man, judging from this.

Mr. McCall directed him how to find the Giant Powder Company's works at Giant, California, on the other side of the Bay, and cautioned him not to get the wrong place. He replied that he knew the Bay, and knew the right place all right.

This man was described as follows:

Age, 32, or thereabouts.

Height, 5 feet 10 or 11 inches.

Weight, 190, or thereabouts.

Face, smooth.

Complexion, sandy.

Eyes, gray or dark blue, one eye (left) had indentation at outer end, might have been from blow.

Hair, sandy and wavy.

Well-built, well-developed chest and shoulders.

Carriage, erect.

Movements, quick and active.

Clothing, dark, of mixed goods, grayish color; sack coat, laydown collar, four-in-hand tie.

Mr. Branson's description tallied with that, and both he and McCall were quite certain they could identify him if they saw him again. Mr. McCall had Mr. Branson look at this man, as his suspicions were aroused slightly, and after he had done so Branson gave the man a receipt for the money paid. Branson also said to McCall at the time, "Take a good look at this man, for we may have to identify him some time. I don't like the look in his eye." Mr. Branson stated that this was the only case in all his experience wherein he had been at all suspicious of a man, and he did not like the manner in which the order was given.

Mr. McCall stated that judging from the man's voice he was the same one that telephoned to him. It was an ordinary male voice and had no peculiarity that he noted.

On Thursday, September 22, this man called again, accompanied by a second man, who was described as follows:

Age, 30 years or thereabouts.

Height, 5 feet 10 inches.

Weight, 160 or 165 pounds.

Build, medium.

Face, smooth.

Features, regular.

Eyes, dark; very black.

Hair, dark.

Clothing, dark material; derby hat.

Appearance, possibly college graduate, used good English, and talked like an educated man.

Both men used good English. No. 1 talked fluently, but No. 2 was not talkative at all. No. 1 stated that he had killed a lot of jack-rabbits while blowing stumps and seemed familiar with the process.

After these men went out, McCall, Branson, and Rennie discussed the matter together, and as No. 1 had stated that the stuff was to be taken to Auburn, California, they arrived at the conclusion that perhaps it was for the purpose of holding up a train and it was decided to notify the special agent of the Southern Pacific Company, and this was at once done. Apparently no attention was paid to this. It had been agreed that the men would call for the stuff next day at the works, and Mr. Wines, of the Southern Pacific Company, Special Agent Department, was personally informed of this, and it was suggested to him that he place men to at least shadow the launch in which these men were to receive the stuff. This was not done as far as we knew.

Mr. Branson went to Sacramento on the river steamer on September 23, the day the launch was to get the stuff, and as the man, No. 1, had stated that he was going up the river to Sacramento with it, in the launch, Mr. Branson was on the lookout all the way up, hoping to see the boat, but he declared that no such boat was to be seen on the river on that date.

On September 22, a telephone call was received at the office of the Giant Powder Company from a man who said: "This is Leonard. I want to get the powder for Bryson. Will I have to get an order?" **Mr.** Rennie, hoping to get a look at the boat, replied that he would take the order down to the boat to him. This man, Leonard, replied: "The boat is now at Sausalito, and I will send my man to you for the order." This was at 1.30 p. m. About 2.30 p. m. a man, whom we shall call No. 3, called at the office of the Giant Powder Company with a letter, which McCall noted had the address, "R. F. D. Auburn," on it. He stated that he had come for the powder for Bryson. His description is given as follows:

Age, 30 to 35 years.

Height, 5 feet 6 inches.

Weight, 140 pounds.

Hair, jet black, straight, smooth, parted in middle and pasted down flat.

Eyes, black and snappy.

Complexion, swarthy.

Features, sharp; deep lines from cheek-bones on both sides, from eyes toward chin.

Shoulders, square.

Clothing, dirty colored gray suit; sack coat; black fedora hat; winged collar; fairly well dressed.

Voice, foreign accent very pronounced.

Stated he was Spanish, and when asked for his name said it was Morris, pronouncing it *Morrice,* with accent on last syllable.

Man No. 3 was asked to describe the size and name of the launch which the goods were to be delivered to, and he stated that he would have to go to Oakland and get this description, as he would see Leonard there. He left, but returned in a short time, too short a time to go to Oakland, and stated that it was a 26-foot launch with a 12-horse power engine, and was named the Peerless. An order was thereupon made out to the works at Giant, Cal., to deliver the stuff, that had been specially made, to the launch Peerless. This was about 4.50 p. m. on September 22.

Mr. Rennie and Mr. McCall talked with man No. 3 until 5.30 p. m., and although he was talkative he was all business, and gave no information that appeared suspicious. He was asked why they wanted such a high-power explosive for the purpose of blowing stumps, and he stated that they also had a large number of hard granite bowlders to blow, and this was why they wanted the high-power stuff. He said: "They are very hard, you know." He appeared familiar with the country in the vicinity of Auburn, where the stuff was supposed to be taken. McCall telephoned the works at Auburn not to deliver the goods to any but the launch Peerless.

About 10.30 or 11 a. m., September 23, this launch, with the three men described above, called at the works at Giant, California, and the stuff was delivered.

CHAPTER IX

AFTER TWO HIRED ANARCHISTS

We had descriptions of "Bryce," "Leonard" and "Morris," and a description of the launch they had used. The boat was found. The owner described the people who had rented it for a cruise and who had put down a deposit of $500 cash for its return in good condition. The launch was named the Peerless, but the dynamiters had renamed it the Pastime.

More descriptions of the three men came along as we looked up every one who had seen them before and after starting away with the launch. The house rented for the storage of the explosive was next found in San Francisco. In the front room under a large canvas cover were ten cases of dynamite. Eight were sewed up in burlap and two were opened. They were all stamped "J. B. Bryson," the name given by the man to the powder company who had first said he was "Bryce." The owner of the house said that he had rented it to a man named William Capp. The description of Capp fitted that of the man who gave the name of Morris, when he called for the dynamite for Bryce or Bryson.

The canvas, covering the boxes of dynamite, bore the name of the maker and I looked him up. He remembered selling it and delivering it to 1565 Grove street. We looked up the address and found that a family named Caplan had occupied a flat there just before the Times explosion and had left immediately afterward. Capp and Caplan were the same and the Caplan was David Caplan, notorious as an Anarchist, his wife being a relative of Emma Goldman. Now we had uncovered somebody. It did not take us long to learn that the man who used the name of Leonard was M. A. Schmidt, another Anarchist, better known as "Schmitty." We found where Schmidt had been rooming and where Bryce had been rooming also. Thus we had located the San Francisco addresses of the three men who had bought the dynamite for the destruction of the Times. The McGraw of the Peoria explosions did not seem to be in on this job. We traced Bryce through many cafés and saloons, found his acquaintances and realized that he was not a native of the Coast. I left him for the men under my son, Raymond, to trail and determined to go after the Anarchists. Caplan and Schmidt were the men I chose to hunt and I did the best I could to take with me on this search a man, who knew Caplan in San Francisco, but was unable to get him to go with me. Therefore, on October 20th, 1910, accompanied by Operative H. A. G. I slipped quietly out of the city, dodging my shadows. We shut ourselves in a stateroom and got under way for Tacoma without anyone knowing that we had left town.

My San Francisco, Los Angeles and Chicago and Indianapolis managers all had their instructions and practically every reliable man of my staff was at work. My stay was to be indefinite.

We hoped to uncover Caplan and Schmidt through watching their friends and fellow Anarchists. Caplan had a wife. Both were known and had lived in the Anarchist settlement of "Home Colony," about twenty miles from Tacoma. While our operatives were seeking them outside we would lie in wait for them or for a letter from either of them inside of the Colony.

In Tacoma I assigned operatives to explore the Anarchist colony in the disguise of engineers and surveyors. They secured maps of the country, equipment for surveying and started off. There had been labor troubles in Seattle and a building had been blown up during the month of August. I started an investigation there among people who handled batteries and found J. D. Waggoner, a teacher in the Trade School of that city who had been called upon by "J. B. Bryce" to instruct him in setting off explosives and sell him a coil for the generation of the spark. Bryce applied for this coil at the shop kept by the teacher. He showed Waggoner a small can containing two sticks of dynamite. On the can was marked "Portland." Waggoner said to Bryce that he did not know that

dynamite was made at Portland. Bryce replied
that it was not Portland, Ore., but Portland, Ind.

Here, then, we had Bryce in Seattle with explosives bought from the very place where "J. B. Mc-
Graw" bought the stuff for the Peoria explosions.
But McGraw and Bryce were not the same people.
Their description did not fit at all. I was then
more confident than ever that the dynamite outrages
all over the country were directed from some headquarters and by some master mind.

In our code we kept the wires hot as the surveillance of the structural iron workers' "leaders"
was carried on in and about Indianapolis.

I returned to Tacoma and directed the search
for the two Anarchists who had assisted Bryce in
his job of blowing the Times to pieces and snuffing
out twenty-one lives.

Home Colony is the nest of Anarchy in the
United States. There are about 1,200 of them
living there without any regard for a single decent
thing in life. They exist in a state of free love, are
notoriously unfaithful to the mates thus chosen and
are so crooked that even in this class of rogues there
does not seem to be any hint of honor.

The Colony did have a post office, but when
McKinley was assassinated the people of this community gave a celebration of the event ending in a
debauch. The Government took the post office away
from them. They do share, however, in the rural
free delivery but the ordinary business of Anarch-

ists is of such a nature that before depositing or receiving a letter, as we later found out, all kinds of precautions were taken to prevent an outsider getting hold of any communication.

In chapters as short as it is possible to make them and to give the public the full picture of Home Colony and its people I shall include the reports of the men I sent there to investigate.

CHAPTER X

WORK IN TACOMA ANARCHIST COLONY

The first report of an operative within the Anarchist colony was sent to me in Tacoma. It was as follows:

"Assistant Manager C. J. S. reports:
"Home Colony, Wash.,
"Friday, November 4th, 1910.

"To-day at 7:30 a. m., in company with Investigator H. J. L., we proceeded to acquaint ourselves with conditions surrounding Home Colony and its residents.

"Our pretext as surveyors permitted us to move around without attracting attention. We found that a number of the community occupy residences in places isolated in the timber and not easy of access. We located the residence of Jay Fox, who is supposed to be connecting with Caplan; also secured a look at Fox and his wife. The home he occupies is so situated that it will be hard to cover without attracting attention. We covered the country thoroughly in the vicinity of Home Colony and found numerous places where Caplan could remain in safe hiding.

"We also noted at what time the rural free delivery at Jay Fox's residence is made by the carrier, so that we can act when the proper time comes.

"I discontinued at 9:00 p. m. without seeing anyone who could answer Caplan's description."

I was then trailing the Fox family in the hope of getting Caplan. I had received information that Caplan had been employed on a paper run by Olaf Tveitmoe. I had reason to believe that Caplan had been employed to assist in the destruction of the Times in Los Angeles. I knew that he was an Anarchist and also knew that he was a friend of Fox. My hope was to get him and get from him a confession.

My operatives in the Anarchist colony continued to report to me day by day and I include their reports here:

"Assistant Manager C. J. S. reports:
        "Home Colony, via Tacoma, Wash.,
                "November 5th, 1910.
"To-day at 7:30 a. m., in company with Investigator H. J. L., I took up a surveillance on the residence of Jay Fox. At 7:45 a. m. he departed, carrying in his hand two letters in large envelopes, proceeding to the boat dock. He gave them to a girl 14 years of age who in turn gave them to a woman evidently her mother who placed them inside of a small hand satchel. As it was evident the

letters had been given to mail in Tacoma, I decided
to keep them under surveillance, as it was evident
that Fox is sending mail outside of the Lake Bay
post office. On arrival in Tacoma, the woman and
girl deposited the letters in a mail box near the
Olympus Hotel.

"Both bore the return address, 'The Agitator,
Lake Bay, Wash.'

"After discussing matters with the informant
relative to future matters of this kind, at 2 :30 p. m.
I departed by boat and returned to Home Colony.
On arrival at 6 :00 p. m. I consulted with Investigator H. J. L. relative to the information developed
during the day, the results of which will be found
embodied in his report for this day.

"I then discontinued."

"Assistant Manager C. J. S. reports:
      "Home Colony, via Tacoma, Wash.,
          "Monday, November 7th, 1910.
"To-day at 7 a. m., in company with Investigator H. J. L., I took up a surveillance on the residence of Jay Fox. At 7 :45 a. m. his son, about
nine years of age, went to the boat-landing with a
bundle of mail and handed it to a woman, who was,
evidently, to mail it in Tacoma. I noticed that
'Blank,' who resides near Jay Fox, and who I had
been informed is not in accord with the socialistic
and anarchistic tendencies of the colony, was also
going to Tacoma on the boat. I decided to leave

with him and also watch the mail carried by the woman, which she had placed in a small bag she carried.

"En route, I discussed matters with 'Blank' and found out that he was bitterly opposed to Jay Fox and his associates. 'Blank' can evidently be used to advantage and is a smart, intelligent man. He intimated that he knew a great deal relative to their movements, which would have a direct bearing on the Los Angeles outrage.

"En route, the woman who was carrying the mail got in touch with an Anarchist named Heyman, a resident of the colony. When they alighted from the boat, I followed the woman, who proceeded to the Tacoma Gas Company's office. Here she opened her hand bag and I noticed that she no longer had this mail, evidently having given it over to Heyman. The latter went to Seattle on the interurban railway. The transfer must have been made on the boat.

"At 2:30 p. m. I returned to Home Colony on the boat, and on arrival at 6 p. m., in company with Investigator H. J. L., I proceeded to Lake Bay, where we consulted with Principal W. J. B. and formulated plans for watching a decoy letter that is to be handled by Jay Fox. During my stay in Tacoma I was in company with 'Blank' who informed me that Jay Fox's wife frequently went to Seattle and frequented a house at 17 Jackson Street, where Anarchists hang out.

"I paved the way for a further interview with 'Blank.' "

"Assistant Manager C. J. S. reports:
  "Home Colony, Wash.,
          "Thursday, November 10th, 1910.
  "To-day at 8:00 a. m., after discussing matters with H. J. L. relative to Jay Fox having mailed four letters through the Lake Bay P. O. that might have some bearing on the Los Angeles case, I departed on the boat and proceeded to Tacoma. On arrival, I called at the Federal Building and consulted with Principal W. J. B.

  "At 2:30 p. m., we departed on the boat. I accompanied Principal W. J. B. to Lake Bay. En route, we discussed matters relative to the delivery of a decoy letter to Jay Fox, which had been arranged for by Principal W. J. B. and plans were formulated to keep this letter under surveillance after it was delivered to Fox.

  "On arrival in Home Colony, I consulted with Investigator H. J. L., and at 9:00 p. m. discontinued."

CHAPTER XI

BURNS SHADOWS THE ANARCHISTS

The reader may or may not understand that the object of our long and tedious work here was not to uncover Anarchy in the United States, but was to get Caplan. We had located his wife and had her under shadow. We knew that he had been in touch with Fox and we expected him to get in touch with him again. I looked for him to show up by letter or in person in Home Colony, and while we covered this end of the case we uncovered the interesting history of the settlement.

Here was my next report from within the lines of the Anarchists:

"Assistant Manager C. J. S. reports:
"Tacoma, Wash., Friday, Nov. 11th, 1910.
"To-day at 7:00 a. m., having learned that the Anarchists were to hold a meeting in Tacoma to-night to commemorate the Haymarket Riot in Chicago, in company with Operative H. J. L., I watched the departure of the Home Colony contingent on the 8:00 a. m. boat. A number of the Anarchists departed but we did not observe Jay Fox among them. His wife, Esther, boarded the

boat. As it was probable that Fox might have proceeded by launch to Steilacoom and had taken the interurban car from there, which would permit him to get in touch with ———, through whom the decoy letter mentioned in yesterday's report is being sent, we proceeded to Lake Bay where we consulted with Principal W. J. B. It was decided that I proceed to Steilacoom by launch and from there go to Tacoma and take up a surveillance of ——— at his place of business in the Fidelity Building. Proceeded to Tacoma. On arrival, I called at the Fidelity Building, where I secured a look at ———. He remained in the room all of the afternoon, neither Fox nor his wife putting in an appearance. At 5:45 p. m. he departed and boarded a car, proceeded to his residence, No. 817 East 11th St. I remained until 9:00 p. m., and as it was evident he intended to remain at home, I then proceeded to the vicinity of the Socialists' hall where the Anarchists' meeting was being held. When the meeting broke up, I saw Mrs. Jay Fox depart in the company of two other women and proceed to the Bodega Hotel. I did not see Fox. Neither did I see anyone answering the description of Caplan depart from the hall.

"At 11:45 p. m. I discontinued."

"Assistant Manager C. J. S. reports:
"Tacoma, Wash., Wednesday, Nov. 16th, 1910.
"To-day at 7:00 a. m., in company with Inves-

tigator H. J. L., I resumed watch on Jay Fox's residence and our information was that Mrs. M., who visited him on yesterday, would go on the boat to Tacoma this morning and might possibly carry the decoy letter. Fox met Mrs. M. and accompanied her to the boat. She departed on same. I followed her. On the boat she met Heyman, the barber, who is a close friend of Fox's. En route, the boat was boarded at Lake Bay by Principal W. J. B. I discussed matters with him and it was decided to keep Heyman also under surveillance.

"On arrival in Tacoma, Heyman and Mrs. M. departed from the boat together and proceeded to Heyman's rooms, 15th and Yakima Ave. They entered at 11:25 a. m. and departed at 12:40 p. m. and proceeded to the corner of 15th and Pacific Ave., where they parted. Mrs. M. was followed by Principal W. J. B. and I kept Heyman under surveillance. He entered the Del Monte Barber Shop, where he is employed, at 15th and Pacific Ave.

"At 1:45 p. m. he departed, proceeding to Andrew's jewelry store, 10th and Pacific Ave., went to the repair department, conversed with the clerk a few minutes and then returned to the Del Monte Barber Shop, remaining until 7:00 p. m.

"He then proceeded to his rooms, 15th and Yakima Ave.

"At 5:45 p. m. I was joined by Principal W. J. B., who assisted me in keeping Heyman under surveillance. At no time did Heyman visit any mail boxes.

"As it was evident that he had received no letters from Jay Fox to mail, I discontinued at 9:00 p. m."

"Investigator H. J. L. reports:
    "Home Colony, Wash., Nov. 5th, 1910.
"This morning at 7:45 a. m., while standing on the porch of Mrs. ———'s home, Assistant Manager C. J. S. and I noticed Jay Fox going toward the boat landing with several letters. We followed him, and upon his arrival he handed them to a young girl about 14 years of age. Fox then left and a few minutes later, and prior to the arrival of the boat, this girl handed them to a lady evidently her mother, and she in turn put them in a small valise she carried. The mother and girl, upon arrival of the boat, boarded same. Assistant Manager C. J. S. accompanied them for the purpose of covering the mail. After the departure of the boat, I returned into the Hills and succeeded in getting acquainted with Mr. Blank, whose home is not far from the Fox home (an excellent place to cover from). I also met Mr. A., who has about the best place here. I ascertained from my landlady that A. is the same class of a man as Fox— an Anarchist. Fox is a free lover; the woman with him is a Jewess. They have two children—a girl about 14 and a boy about 12 years. The children I became acquainted with at my boarding house.

They were soliciting subscriptions for the paper edited by their father.

"I purchased a copy. Fox took part in the Haymarket Riot in Chicago. I have also received information that this paper is printed in the town here, in what is known as the Old Colony Hall. This is a large two story frame building about a half mile from the Fox house. The windows are all boarded up. I understand they have four rooms there. They are using an old style Washington hand press and three or four men are working in there. We are getting acquainted very nicely, going along very slowly and feeling our way and the cover is first class. We have created no suspicion. Tomorrow we will see what we can learn as to conditions around the building where the print shop is. I have become acquainted with the three store keepers, all friendly and will talk."

CHAPTER XII

DETECTIVES IN THE RED COLONY

So far none of my operatives had aroused any suspicion. They had made good in "covering" themselves in their work. I, myself, was able to go in and out of the colony at times without creating suspicion. My operatives reported to me daily and I show their reports.

"H. J. L. reports:
"Home Colony, via Tacoma, November 7th, 1910.
"I resumed investigation here this morning at 7:00 a. m. At 8:00 a. m. Mr. 'Blank' departed on the steamer for Tacoma. I introduced Assistant Manager C. J. S. to him and C. J. S. accompanied him to Tacoma. The latter lives near the Jay Fox residence and should be in possession of some information. The rest of the morning up to 12:00 noon, I walked through the Colony getting acquainted with the inhabitants. I ascertained that Emma Goldman was here, but how lately I could not learn, I believe, however, very recently. She is a great friend of the mother of 'my landlady.' Her parents and grandfather, so she states, are Anarchists,

Socialists, free lovers and all that goes with it. Elbert Hubbard was also here.

"This evening, there arrived on the boat, a Mr. D., who was decorated with a Western Federation of Miners' button, an Industrial Worker of the World button, also a Socialist button. He announced himself as an Anarchist and all that goes with it. He claims to be from Siskiyou County, California, and is lecturing around the country on Socialism, the down-trodden workingman,—'God's patient poor,' etc. He is very inquisitive. He brought his trunk with him; states that he may stay a day, or maybe a month. He is one of the Emma Goldman type.

"Between 12:00 and 1:00 to-day, I covered the Fox printing shop from the brush; saw him leave there and go to his home for dinner and also return. His print shop is in the same building as the public school. The two school teachers are Mr. Allen and his wife; Allen is an Anarchist and, as I mentioned in a previous report, is a great friend of Fox.

"This afternoon, I went into the hills and followed a course that led me into several abandoned houses or cabins. Upon my return, I remained about the stores, as this seems to be trading day. At 5:00 p. m. I received word to come to Lake Bay to see Principal W. J. B. Assistant Manager C. J. S. returned from Tacoma and after supper we walked to Lake Bay, met Principal W. J. B.,

received additional instructions, returned to Home
Colony and discontinued at 9:30 p. m.

"Our actions are creating no suspicion here; we
have seen most of the residents here and know them
by sight."

My visits to the Colony of Anarchists became
more frequent. I was always hopeful of getting
Caplan. Dressed in hunting costume, I tramped
in and around the Colony, conferred with my operatives and kept after the man I wanted most. It
was while engaged in this work that I got from my
son, Raymond J. Burns, manager of my Chicago
office, that Mayor Alexander at Los Angeles had
been stopped from paying me any more money
until I had obtained results. I had no intention of
giving away my case to anyone and Mayor Alexander understood that thoroughly. He had promised me that he would not give any reports of mine
to anyone.

The Mayor was asked to submit my reports, and
when he refused a Grand Jury was called. Mr.
Rodgers was appointed an Assistant District Attorney. The Mayor was subpœnaed before the Grand
Jury and was there urged to submit my reports.
On the failure to secure them from him, the manager of my Los Angeles office was called before the
Grand Jury, and he too was unable to produce
them; and that night my Los Angeles office was
broken into, and the filing-cases and desks rifled.

But their search was fruitless, as all the reports in this case were forwarded to my son, Raymond J. Burns, at Chicago, and he, in turn, placed them in a safe deposit vault in the First National Bank.

CHAPTER XIII

BURNS IN ANARCHISTS' NEST

These annoyances were big annoyances and they hampered me somewhat in my work, but as long as there was a chance to get Caplan in Home Colony or break out a trail to him there I was going to stick. I financed myself—and borrowed money to pull through with the job. We kept at the job as the following reports in the files of my agency will show.

"H. J. L. reports:
        "Home Colony, via Tacoma, Wash.,
                "Tuesday, November 5th, 1910.
"I resumed investigation here to-day at 7:00 a. m. covering the outgoing boat to Tacoma to ascertain whether Fox sent out any mail. Assistant Manager C. J. S. left for Tacoma on the boat. My informant has given me the following information:
"Fox worked in San Francisco for some time up to within two months ago, when he returned here and made arrangements to start up his paper, The Agitator. For a long time past, Fox has had the residents here subscribing money for this paper and

has given them nothing in return. The money so subscribed, so the residents here claim, has gone to 'Esther.'

"This woman has lived with him ten years. She was formerly the wife of a wealthy New York dentist. The boy and girl who are here now are the children of her husband in New York.

"Fox has a wife and children living. Whether Fox followed the printing trade in San Francisco, I was unable to ascertain. He did have a job as watchman at the Seattle fair, a year ago.

" 'D,' the party who arrived last night, visited Fox to-day; also Mrs. V., the mother of our landlady. D. is a 'faker.' He came here looking for the 'free love' end of it. I am satisfied of that. He spent but little time with Fox, remaining all day and evening at the home of Mrs. V. He is going to leave in the morning, and Assistant Manager C. J. S. will take him into Tacoma.

"I am going to try and ascertain where Fox lived in San Francisco. In a previous report, I mentioned that Fox was in the Haymarket Riots in Chicago.

"The lady who handled the letters for Fox on the steamer Monday was Mrs. B., an Englishwoman, who lives on a remittance and also writes for the magazines. She has a husband here. They are divorced. She rents a house here, and stays two or three days out of the week here, and while here, she and others of the 'free love' faith hold a drunken carnival.

"The Jewish tailor, F., is pretty sore at the Fox family and might have some information."

"H. J. L. reports:
    "Home Colony, via Tacoma, Wash.,
        "Saturday, November 12th, 1910.
"I resumed operations here at 6:30 a. m. and joined Principal W. J. B. at 7:30 a. m. at Lake Bay, remained with him until 9:00 a. m. and re-joined him at 10:15 a. m. at the home of his informant at Home Colony. Principal W. J. B., informant and I then went to an abandoned cabin a short distance from the house. Informant told Principal W. J. B. that in the latter part of either July or August, 1910, he had a conversation with one E., the manager of the Home Grocery Company here. E. is a great friend of Jay Fox. E. told informant that he had something on his mind and was going to tell him his secret. Informant showed no anxiety in the matter and consequently E. only told part of the secret which in effect was as follows:

"That he (E.) feared for the safety of Fox; that Fox was going in with some fellows on a dangerous job, and the consequence would be that Fox would get caught and be made to suffer, while the others would go free. Fox, at this time, was in a bad way financially, being so hard pressed for cash that he had to have E. extend credit to him for a sack of flour. In the latter part of August a Jew

came to visit Fox. He stayed several days and
was with Fox constantly. He stayed so close to
him that E. had no chance at all to talk with him.
He told informant he wanted to talk with Fox and
see if he could not persuade him to keep out of
anything that would lead him into trouble. About
September 1st, the Jew and Fox left for San Francisco. Fox's wife left shortly before this. Was
supposed to go to Portland. On October the 6th,
Fox returned alone from San Francisco. He was
met on the steamer by informant. Informant reports the condition of Fox as follows: Very much
worried; eyes blood-shot; looked as though he had
been under a great strain. About two weeks after
he returned, his wife appeared at Home Colony.

"From that part of the 'secret' that E. told informant, E. is in possession of valuable information.
No doubt Fox made a confidant of him and looked
to him for advice. E. states he advised him to
keep out of it. Possibly, Fox heeded that advice
for the time being, but when the mysterious Jew
appeared, Fox, three or four days after, accompanied him to San Francisco. He had money shortly
after he bought the flour on credit. He paid his
bill and Mrs. Fox had money to go to Portland on.
On last Saturday, the first issue of his paper, The
Agitator, came out. He has one man working for
him.

"Since the dynamiting at Los Angeles, informant
at different times has attempted to draw E. out on

the matter and to learn the secret that he at one time wanted to tell him. E. has 'shut up completely and informant can learn nothing from him. Principal W. J. B. advised informant how to handle E. in the future. E. has always been a rank Anarchist until lately. He is not as strong as formerly. Principal W. J. B. gave informant and myself instructions as to how to handle the situation in the future. He left us at 11:45 a. m.

"I then had a further conference with informant, went to dinner and then met him at E.'s store. Informant and I discussed the surveying of some land in order to throw off any suspicions on the part of E.

"Mrs. Fox is supposed to go to Seattle this trip to have an operation performed upon her daughter's throat.

"As stated before, there is no question but what E. has the confidence of Fox and knows the details of the Los Angeles crime. He tried to keep Fox from mixing in it, but when Fox did get mixed into it, he used every precaution to shield him.

"This evening at 7:00 p. m. I went to Lake Bay and joined Principal W. J. B. and Assistant Manager C. J. S. We discussed matters fully and discontinued at 11:30 p. m."

CHAPTER XIV

WITH NO LAW AND NO MORALS

"H. J. L. reports:

"Home Colony, via Tacoma, Washington,
"Sunday, November 15th, 1910.

"I left Lake Bay at 9:00 a. m. with Assistant Manager C. J. S., consulting with Principal W. J. B. before leaving. Fox returned from Tacoma last night alone. Did not get to see him at all to-day, but am satisfied from investigation made by Assistant Manager C. J. S. and myself he was at his home. We covered outgoing Tacoma-bound steamer, but he sent no mail out. The following are the fixed and definite dates as regards the movements of Fox prior to his departure for San Francisco, September 2nd, 1910.

"Fox at E.'s house all day, September 3rd, 1910. E. sent for informant. This is the time he stated he had a secret he wanted to tell (see my report of November 12th, 1910); September 4th, the Jew (see report of November 12th, 1910) and Fox left for San Francisco; October 6th, 1910, Fox returned from San Francisco; seen on steamer plying between Tacoma and Home Colony by informant. Description of one Joe Edelson, who came to the

'Home' in the spring of 1910, and occupied a cabin near the home of Fox.

"Five feet 8 inches, 35 or 36 years, very dark complexion, black hair, black eyes, eyes beady; 130 to 135 pounds, Jewish nationality.

"Left 'Home' in the early part of June, 1910, and went to Portland; remained there during the Rose Carnival, then returned here, remained a short time and left for Los Angeles, where he is now, living with some woman. Edelson is a great friend of Fox and is an Anarchist.

"To-day being Sunday, we loitered around the stores, as here it is where most of the residents congregate."

"H. J. L. reports:
"Home Colony, via Tacoma, Washington,
"Monday, November 14th, 1910.

"I resumed investigation here at 7:00 a. m. Assistant Manager C. J. S. went to Lake Bay, and I remained here to cover the 8:00 a. m. Tacoma-bound steamer to see if Fox sent out any mail by any of the passengers. He did not, and I rode the steamer as far as Lake Bay. Upon reaching there, I met Assistant Manager C. J. S. and he stated that he was going to Tacoma with Principal W. J. B.

"I then returned to Home Colony, located Jay Fox in his home and then saw informant and remained with him until 11:45 a. m.

"At 1:00 p. m. I returned to the vicinity of the Fox home and remained in the timber until 4:00 p. m. when I left for Lake Bay.

"There is a woman living in San Francisco, Cal., who formerly lived here. Her name is ———, and her address ———. Her age is about 30, dark, small in build; a Jewess. She is living with an Anarchist named ———. Both are rank Anarchists and very friendly to the Fox family. Possibly M., a cousin of the woman, is living with them. These people left here the latter part of July, 1910, for San Francisco. If Fox was in San Francisco he most likely visited them."

Here my operative gave a complete list of the most violent of the Anarchists in the Colony. It is necessary for me to keep this information secret. Some of the immoralities of these people, recounted in the reports of my men, are not printed for decency's sake.

But here is one fact in this operative's report that may be worth while printing:

"John B. is the butcher here. He has very strong Anarchistic views. At the time President McKinley was shot, B. was a resident of a small town near Seattle. When the news of the assassination reached the town, B. was very much elated and declared himself. The consequences were that a rope was put around his neck and he escaped lynching

by a very narrow margin. He says: 'That was
the way I was treated in what they call a "free
country."' "

How close we were in the heart of this Colony
of law-hating people will be shown in this report,
the last I will include in this phase of my chronicles.

"H. J. L. reports:
"Home Colony, via Tacoma, Wash.,
"Tuesday, November 15th, 1910.
"I resumed investigation at 6:30 a. m. At 7:30
a. m. I went to informant's house and concealed
myself in the loft of the stable where I had an
excellent opportunity to observe the Fox home and
the movements of Fox. Informant remained with
me all day and until I discontinued for supper.
After supper we took up separate watches in the
timber surrounding the Fox home. Fox is building
a small addition to his home and is putting in a new
floor. He did not leave the house at all except to
go to the mail box for his mail.

"7:30 a. m.—I took up watch in stable loft.
"9:00 a. m.—Mail carrier arrived—left mail in
box.
"9:15 a. m.—A. arrived at Fox's home.
"9:50 a. m.—Mrs. ——— arrived at Fox's
home.
"10:05 a. m.—Mrs. ——— left Fox's home.
"10:40 a. m.—Fox came to mail box, then started

in a hurry toward the ——— home. Informant trailed him and reported that Fox walked around the block, hurriedly opened one of the letters, looked at it for a few seconds and then returned to his home.

"10:45 a. m.—Mrs. ——— arrived at Fox's home.

"11:05 a. m.—Mrs. ——— left Fox's home.

"11:45 a. m.——————, a neighbor, arrived at Fox's home.

"1:00 p. m.—Mrs. ——— arrived at Fox's home.

"1:00 p. m.—A. came out of Fox's home to road, returned to house immediately.

"1:10 p. m.—A. left Fox home with small package under his arm; started on road toward Lake Bay.

"1:12 p. m.—Mrs. ——— left Fox home.

"1:35 p. m.—B. left Fox home.

"4:30 p. m.—Mrs. ——— arrived at Fox home.

"4:35 p. m.—Mrs. ——— left Fox home.

"5:30 p. m.—Man, 5 feet 8 inches, 155 pounds, arrived with two packages. It was getting dark and neither informant nor I could identify him as being anyone living in the Colony. At 5:30 p. m. this party left.

"At 6:30 p. m. I joined informant again, remained with him in timber until 7:30 p. m. Assistant Manager C. J. S. joined me and we watched Fox's home until 11:30 p. m. I discontinued at midnight. Fox remained in house; no one called.

"After arrival of mail, Fox did not deposit any outgoing mail in letter box; neither did he give any to carrier who passed his house at 11:30 a. m. As will be noted, Mrs. —— called four times. I understand she is going to Tacoma in the morning. Mrs. —— has a home here. Her husband is not here, but sends her a check every month to the amount of $50.00.

"After A. left at 1:10 p. m. Fox practically discontinued his carpenter work and all was quiet around the house. I understand that within the last week the two Fox children changed a twenty dollar gold piece (that is, each child had one) at the Colony store. Regarding E. mentioned in former reports, he and the tailor of Tacoma were very friendly. The tailor visited him here. E. was a peddler of notions, women's goods, etc. He was a loud-mouthed Jew and a strong Anarchist. My informant tells me, he answers the description of Caplan, as to height, color and age."

We trailed Anarchist E., but he was not the man I wanted.

CHAPTER XV

A $350 TAXICAB RIDE

Despite these interesting adventures in the Anarchist City we did not get close enough to Caplan or Schmidt to either rope them or arrest them. To rope a man is to gain his full confidence and that is even better than an arrest, as will appear later in the reports of the operatives who closed in on Bryce and McGraw in another part of the country.

We found Mrs. Caplan and, up to the very moment of the McNamara trial, when the two defendants pleaded guilty, we had strong hopes of getting her husband. My operatives relieved me of this puzzling end of the case as my attention was needed in a general direction of the investigation as clues were dug out and the trail to the guilty men became wider and straighter.

Even after the close of the trial two investigators followed two men answering the descriptions of Caplan and Schmidt through barren and remote parts of the west, followed them on foot, on horseback and raced after them in automobiles finally to round them up and to find that they were not the right men.

As for Mrs. Caplan, that lady was destined to

enjoy a taxicab ride the like of which few Anarchist ladies have ever dreamed of enjoying, but the ride was not at the expense of my agency. Mr. Olaf Tveitmore, secretary of the California State Building Trades Council, sometimes known among labor people on the Coast as "The Old Man," later indicted and convicted for conspiracy, had a hand in providing this record taxi trip. The bill for Mrs. Caplan's trip was $350, as much as a laborer makes in a year, and the misguided union working-man who paid his dues regularly footed the bill, of course.

Mrs. Caplan was under subpœna in San Francisco. The service of the subpœna on the woman made agents for the McNamara defense believe that the best thing that could happen would be her disappearance. Elaborate plans were laid and one day in August, 1911, she stepped into a machine and was gone. She was taken to San José first and then on to Reno, where she was piled aboard a Chicago express without bag or baggage. The machine turned about and crossed the country again to San Francisco and its garage. It had required two days going to Reno and three days returning. A good part of a thousand dollars went for this little joy ride of an Anarchist lady if the railroad fare from Reno to Chicago and incidentals are included. She was not really needed by the prosecution. Her husband was the one we were after. It was money thrown away.

Of course our investigators learned every detail of this spiriting away of the witness and, incidentally, we got hold of the chauffeur and secured a statement from him. We learned a lot about taxi bills, money provided by honest union men who were being bled by the conspirators. We learned that "The Old Man," Tveitmore, who was charged with directing the explosions on the Pacific Coast, seldom walked. He always used a taxi and a certain special taxi and a certain chauffeur. This same chauffeur also saved Mr. Sam Gompers from ever stretching his legs and was at the beck and call of Clarence Darrow, Job Harriman, Harrington, Rappaport and the rest of the crowd that assembled around Tveitmore in San Francisco prior to the trial. Everybody used a taxi except the man on the job with a dinner pail. Yet the man on the job paid the bills.

Chicago, to which city Mrs. Caplan made her flight, seems to be a good hiding place for Anarchists when they stir about the country from their home places. Schmidt used it as a good point for receiving information that would guide him in dodging us and, perhaps, for receiving necessary funds. We uncovered his mail agent, a young man we shadowed for many days. We had our best shadow assigned to this young man, Malcolm McLaren, an operative who figures largely later in this chronicle. How cautious Anarchists are will be shown by the manner in which Schmidt's mail was handled. Schmidt's agent asked at the Chicago general delivery office every night for mail for M. A. Schmidt. The round-about course he would take in doing this service for the Anarchist would have done credit to a fox. To obey my standing instructions in shadowing, McLaren must have had his patience tried sorely at times, for one of the big reasons for the successful work of my agency is that the moment a subject shows that he knows that he is being followed the shadow must draw off. Never mind how promising may be the outlook, my men are ordered to sacrifice all the good chances rather than let the subject know that a shadow is behind him. Later the subject will be taken up again by another man and the work started all over.

McLaren was watching this subject's house on the afternoon of December 28, 1910, when the subject came out at four o'clock. His report says that Schmidt's agent proceeded east on Eastwood Avenue, Chicago, to the Robey Street elevated station. He boarded an express train for downtown and got off at State and Van Buren Streets. He entered Rothschild's department store and bought a key ring. Then he popped out of the store and for three minutes stood on the corner looking in every direction. Suddenly he turned and ascended the elevated stairs to the sub-platform. He passed from the north side to the south side and stood there about two minutes, watching. He then returned to the street and hurried to Clark Street and to the post office. He went to the employees' entrance but did not inquire at the general delivery window for Schmidt's mail that day. This young man, interested in Anarchists, seldom left his home by the front door but used a rear entrance and gained the main highways of the city by alleys. It would require a stretch of the imagination to believe that his life was a pleasant one or one offering him much promise in manhood.

During this unsuccessful work among the Anarchists, my operatives were exceedingly busy in Los Angeles, San Francisco, Chicago, Indianapolis and Salt Lake City. In the last named city there was a gentleman named Munsey—Jack Munsey—who needed attention. He was the business agent or walking delegate for the International Bridge and Structural Iron Workers' Union. We had reason to believe that "J. B. Bryce" would get in touch with him. Munsey had been known by another name and had a none too pretty reputation. Our operative reported that his wife had divorced him and that he was loafing about Salt Lake City with plenty of money all the time while the union workers in the craft were kept on strike and were so reduced in funds that they got down to borrowing small change from each other to tide over each day. He was among those to be convicted later at Indianapolis.

We had reason to believe that Munsey would provide a cover for Bryce, the man who had actually set off the dynamite in the Los Angeles Times Building. Our operative stuck with him and reported among other things a hold-up proposition from him in the matter of getting work; if there was work to be had the iron-worker would have to pay over a tidy lump sum to Munsey before swinging a sledge or picking up a piece of iron on the job.

We got some helpful information there and then things began to center closely around headquarters in Indianapolis. I learned that a man fitting the description of McGraw had been seen talking with J. J. McNamara. I finally spotted McGraw and from the time he came within our vision he was never without a shadow day or night. He it was who led us to the men higher up—the two McNamaras and all the crew back of them.

McGraw had had nothing to do with the Los Angeles Times explosion, but he had done the work in Peoria and how many other places we did not know at that time. Our shadows followed him and finally he went to his home, No. 414 South Sangamon Street, Chicago. There we got his true identity. He was Ortie McManigal. In the subsequent account of the trailing, or "tailing" of McManigal as we call it, he is referred to as Subject No. 1.

CHAPTER XVI

TRACKED TO WILDS OF WISCONSIN

On the morning of November 5th, 1910, an expressman stopped in front of this subject's house, entered the alley adjoining and, a few moments later, returned with a small trunk. Later the subject appeared, wearing corduroy trousers, a long black ulster and a soft black felt hat. He carried three shotguns in cases. He took a train to Kenosha, Wis., and in that city went to the house of G. M. Sharp, a carpenter, at No. 620 Exchange Street. He left his guns there and reappeared with Sharp. They went to the station and waited for the 3:55 train from Chicago. They were suspicious of every one, but did not uncover the shadows. On the arrival of the train a passenger alighted and greeted them. This passenger went under the name of Sullivan. He is referred too hereafter as Subject No. 2.

Hunting licenses were secured for Subjects 1 and 2 and several others making up a party of six. Trunks were sent to the station and one of our operatives took the job of following them in the event that the shadow following the subjects became uncovered.

The hunters boarded a train for Conover, Wis., our men following on the next train after being sure that Conover was the destination of the party. This was only a month and nine days after the destruction of the Los Angeles Times and the papers were still filled with the aftermath of the horror. The dynamiters were going into seclusion until things simmered down. It would be harder to find more seclusion than in the wilds of Wisconsin in winter.

In Conover Operatives B. F. D. and R. J. K. found that the refugee hunters had landed there and had gone into camp near Pioneer Lake, two and one half miles east of the road leading into Conover. They sought a distant telegraph station and wired Chicago, making a report. They then bought the equipment necessary for a hunting trip, fur caps, snowshoes, guns, etc., and arranged a story between them to the effect that they were purchasers of mining machinery, waiting for its arrival and killing time until it was delivered. They had a hunting license, bought provisions and rented a cabin which they put in repair so that they could stand the weather with a reasonable degree of comfort.

The cabin of the two operatives was near the Conover station, so chosen because here was the general store to which hunters would make their way for provisions and ammunition and to mail and receive letters. My men could also watch all arriving and departing trains, keep track of all people leaving or coming to Conover and also watch the delivery of express packages and mail.

On the morning of November 12th, 1910, Subjects 1 and 2 came into Conover from their camp. Subject 1—McManigal—told of having killed a two hundred and fifty pound buck, bringing him down with one shot. Subject 2—known as Sullivan —was dressed in a dark corduroy suit, high-laced hunting boots and light corduroy cap. Both were armed with high power rifles and 44 caliber Colts. The two men bought some bottled beer and provisions and then hired the section foreman to take them on a hand car to a point near the camp. The assistant of the foreman, a man named Tony, went with the party on the hand car and on the return of Tony our operatives made friends with him. Our operatives took their meals at a house near the station where Tony ate. The arrangement was that pending closer contact with the men they were tailing in the wilds of Wisconsin, Tony could keep our operatives posted.

The arrival of some baggage at the station put our men on edge a week later. It looked as if the subjects under surveillance were preparing to depart. The Chicago office was informed and men were in readiness to pick up the subjects wherever they went. The office received a telegram, however, from B. F. D. reading:

"Tell B. not to ship machinery to-day."

This was to inform us that the subjects were not leaving.

The task of shadowing men in camp in the woods was no easy one. Our operatives scouted the roads about the camp and one of them got so far as to aid a farmer named Reed in carting McManigal's deer to the station and unloading it. He and Reed made friends and what Reed knew of the life in the camp of the dynamiters my men got out of him. Then, again, like most women, Mrs. Steinmetz, who took table boarders at Conover, generally knew what was happening for miles around. Her daughter, Mrs. Nicholson, also generally heard what was being talked about. They informed my men that the camp of the subjects would be broken in about a week from November 24th and that all would depart save Sullivan, who was to board with her until the close of the hunting season.

On November 26th, Sullivan reached a high point in a spree that had been gradually developing. He came into Conover with a rifle and a pail in either hand and went to the Steinmetz house. He was pretty drunk and my men did not hang about too close for fear that they might meet him and he might get suspicious of them. Operative B. remained about our cabin to watch Sullivan and also the trains so that none of the party would get away without it being known to them. Sullivan's debauch continued at the Steinmetz house and he spent twenty dollars in drinks for everyone and divided five dollars among the children. The drunk wound up with a free fight between Steinmetz, Mrs. Steinmetz, a man named Sam Smiley, several of the children and such friends of the family who cared to join in. Sullivan was so far gone in drink that he rolled over on the kitchen floor in the midst of battle and slept peacefully. Later he was put to bed. The next morning our men went to the Steinmetz house for breakfast and found Sullivan still drunk and asleep in a chair in the front room. The operatives were working with the greatest of caution. They decided that some of the others from the camp would come for the drunken man and so they withdrew to the woods, spending the forenoon of November 27th in watching the roads leading from the station. At noon they returned to the house but Sullivan was still there. Operative B. was in charge of our cabin while the other two men watched the roads. In the afternoon Subject 1—McManigal—came into Conover from the camp to get Sullivan. Sullivan brought McManigal to our cabin and knocked on the door, demanding to see "Billy," Operative B.

The roping of the two subjects was now well under way. Instead of seeking acquaintance with them they were hunting us up. The acquaintance-ship with our party was made. Operatives and subject had dinner together at the Steinmetz house and the subjects talked of their camp life and the game they had killed. They said they would break

camp the next Friday night, come to Conover, spend
the night there and leave for Chicago in the morning. This was most important information for us
for we then had time to prepare to pick them up
when they left the train on the way back to civilization.

One detail of their task which was important and
which might have been overlooked by less careful
detectives was efficiently attended to by the operatives at Conover. The hunting laws there provide
that when deer is shipped the hunter must accompany it to its destination. The killed deer were
watched almost as closely as the hunters themselves
for the delivery of the game would mean another
name and address, a friend of the men under surveillance and a new avenue for investigation.

The intended breaking up of the camp was post-
poned and Manager Raymond J. Burns was so
notified by wire in his Chicago office. This gave
our operatives greater opportunity for roping the
subjects. Subject No. 2 was by no means through
with his debauch. He would get totally drunk, try
to taper off and then find himself drunk again.
Everything to drink in the Steinmetz house was
used up and Mrs. Steinmetz on a trip to Eagle
River, a nearby station, bought a bottle of whiskey
for Sullivan which she agreed to drop him when
the train passed Scott station. Sullivan was waiting
for it and Mrs. Steinmetz dropped it from the train.
Somebody's hand was unsteady and the bottle hit

the ground and the much coveted liquor was wasted.

Sullivan, while in the Steinmetz house, played the part of a ladies' man when he was sober enough to do so. He scolded Tessie Steinmetz for only baking two loaves of bread and the girl was resentful and called him a brute. But he had plenty of money, more money than the people around Conover were used to seeing, and Mrs. Steinmetz tried to keep peace in the family.

It was soon after the spat with the girl that the general ruction came off in the Steinmetz family. The report of Operative B. on this social affair may prove interesting. It is very brief and is as follows:

"Operative B. reports:

"Conover, Wis., Nov. 26th, 1910.

"At nine in the morning Sullivan came to Conover alone, carrying a .203 Savage carbine and a small pail. He went to the post office and store where he ordered some provisions. He then went to the Steinmetz residence and ordered a round of drinks and by ten o'clock was very drunk. Rempert, the section foreman, had promised to take him back to his camp. At 2:30 p. m. one of the parties from the house and I returned home and when within one hundred yards Alice and Marguerite Steinmetz, 15 and 16 years of age, came running out of the house crying at the tops of their voices. Everyone in the store and post office ran out to see what was the matter. The girls ran for me and told me that everybody in the house was fighting and that Sullivan had drawn his revolver. I ran into the house, entering through the sitting-room, as I knew they were in the kitchen. I remained in the dining-room and looked through the window into the kitchen and saw Mrs. Steinmetz receive a blow in the jaw from Sullivan as she was holding her husband. Sullivan also punched him in the jaw and ear, cutting both places. Sullivan was very drunk. He then rolled over on the floor for a nap. At 4:30 the section foreman pulled out the hand car to take Sullivan back to his camp. He got him to the station but he fell forward on his face, making his nose bleed. He went back to the Steinmetz house. He was taken upstairs and put to bed."

Operative B., who was now called "Billy" by the man he was shadowing, showed up early the next morning and found Sullivan starting a new spree. He was buying drinks for the people he had been fighting the day before.

Two of the Steinmetz lodgers and Sullivan then went over to the cabin of my operatives to finish up the spree. They brought along beer and made themselves comfortable. Operative B. suggested to Sullivan that it was a good thing that his partners were not in Conover during the fight the day before.

"If Mac was here," replied Sullivan, "there would have been something doing because he always carries his Colt automatic just as I do. Most of the time, even in the city, he carries two guns with him, and if he only has one with him he carries a large dagger. He runs no chances and whenever he pulls the trigger his man falls. He is a conservative fellow, can scent trouble, is always prepared and has never lost out yet. He can put a piece of paper as large as your hand on a tree and at twenty-five paces can put nine out of ten bullets in the center."

Charlie Lawrence, another member of the party, was described by Sullivan as being "nobody's bud" and the "gamest kid in the country." He also carried two Colt revolvers and was a quick shot. He said that wherever they were they carried an extra clip of eight cartridges.

This was not all drunken talk by any means. The bunch of men my operatives were tailing could stand off in the road and roll a tomato can along with the bullets from their guns. Had there been any suspicion that the operatives were Burns men and not hunters and mining men, had there been the slightest careless work on the part of my investigators they would have had to battle with their own weapons for their lives. The two subjects were wanted for murder in connection with the Los Angeles Times explosion and they would not have hesitated to put up a battle with rifles and pistols.

Operative B. wanted a photograph of Sullivan. The Chicago office would have given almost anything for one so that they might check up on the subject and definitely prove his identity. In one of B.'s reports there is a good description of how he went about getting or trying to get a picture of Sullivan. Along with this description of the attempt to get the picture are more details of the life in the little railway station where two men wanted for murder and two men shadowing them spent the heart of the winter of 1910. In this report "Subject" refers to McManigal.

From report of Operator B.:

"Sullivan is a great ladies' man and is trying hard to win two of the girls here. He invited me to his camp several times, and were it not for the house running out of beer and whiskey, he would have told me a lot more. He seems worried and told me he has lost about ten pounds in the last month but passed it off by saying he guessed he wasn't drinking enough out here.

"Several of the girls from the town here were talking to me from about 200 feet away and he asked me to invite them over, which I did and I told them I wanted to take their pictures, and having a plate camera which I had borrowed in the morning, I lined up the girls and several children and Park and Sullivan, but Sullivan refused to get in the picture and insisted on operating the camera himself telling me he had one of the finest cameras made at his camp and it cost him $60.00 and that when I came to his camp, we would have some good photos taken.

"It was raining all day and very dark, but Sullivan insisted that I could take a good 'time' photo. One of the girls wanted a photo of a little two-year-old girl and while Sullivan held her in his arms I took the picture and will send the three plates in to be developed to-morrow, although I doubt if any will turn out O. K.

"At 5 p. m. the subject came to Conover carrying a .303 Savage rifle, and also carried a .38 Colt automatic revolver and one eight-inch blade dagger at his side and carried two pockets of cartridges. He first went to the post office and then returned to the Steinmetz house where he met Sullivan and they talked about fifteen minutes in the front room, then both went into the kitchen where they had several drinks of the last pint of whiskey in the house, while Mrs. Steinmetz and others told the subject of the fight of yesterday. The subject joked about it and said he would have to keep Sullivan in camp for the rest of the week.

"Sullivan and the subject went over to the store and purchased a lot of groceries, etc., and then went over to my cabin looking for me, and one half hour later I heard Operative R. J. K. talking and not knowing the subject and Sullivan were in my cabin I walked in on them, and they were sitting on the beds talking to Operatives B. F. D. and R. J. K. and a fellow named Tony, who was out hunting with them. They had several bottles of beer that they managed to get somewhere. T. took sides with Sullivan, explaining the fight of yesterday and the subject seeing that Sullivan and I were very friendly, the subject changed from general conversations to stories and finally we were all called over to dinner. The subject, Sullivan, Operatives R. J. K. and B. F. D., Tony from Eagle River and I dined together, and after dinner returned to the sitting room. Sullivan was still drunk and would not take Mrs. Steinmetz's word that there was no more booze in the house, but went into the cellar to see for himself, then brought the jug of rootbeer and treated the house with it.

"Operative R. J. K. told the subject he was from Milwaukee and they talked together for about half an hour. While the subject, Sullivan and all the rest of us were in the sitting-room after dinner, the subject told us he used to spend about six months out of every year hunting and trapping; that he would go and hunt for a month or so then return to the city and work for a month and keep that up month after month.

"The subject and Sullivan both asked Operatives B. F. D. and R. J. K. and I to their camp next Wednesday night and we told them we would be there."

The next morning the operatives made a definite engagement for a visit to the camp of the dynamiters and they ordered a case of beer shipped ahead of them. It was not, by any means, a perfectly safe venture, for one of the dynamiters carried a Maxim silencer on the barrel of his rifle and took pains to suggest that he could shoot and it would be almost impossible to hear the report a hundred feet away.

A blizzard on the day appointed for the visit to the camp brought about a postponement and gave us an opportunity to send another operator to Conover with instructions to the men already on the spot. We also sent a kodak to replace the camera of Operative B., in the hope that he would get a chance for a snapshot. The additional operative was introduced at the Steinmetz house as a salesman for the Allis-Chalmers Company. Operatives R. J. K., B. F. D. and B. then arranged a telegraphic code with him and hustled him out of Conover to Monica Junction, some distance away.

The bad weather kept up and on December 2nd, the camp of the subjects was broken, all parties coming into Conover. No. 1—McManigal— bossed them all and several times called Sullivan and others from the Steinmetz house and gave them a talking to for drinking. McManigal could drink and carry it but Sullivan got very drunk again. Sullivan wanted to sleep in our shack with B., but McManigal would not let him.

In Chicago we were ready for the tailing of the members of the camp as they left the woods of

Wisconsin. Spotters were ready to point out each subject and shadows ready to tail them.

On the morning of December 3rd McManigal tried to get Sullivan to leave Conover with him, but Sullivan was still drunk and insisted on remaining. He was very much worried and advised Sullivan, who is to be referred to in reports following as "Subject 2," to keep away from people and not to talk. He seemed to be afraid that No. 2 would tell things. McManigal went away with others of the party, one of our shadows tailing them and sending information ahead.

Not knowing when Subject 2 would pick up and leave, B. had a telegram sent him which would serve as an excuse and head off suspicion that he was following his man. This telegram read: "For over thousand dollar purchase you must arrange with our Mr. Hayden for special discount. He leaves for East Monday. (Signed) Harris."

After the departure of Subjects 1 and 3, Operative B. wired Operative R. J. K. at Milwaukee: "Order size one and three Eye Steam pumps of Allis-Chalmers Co., in Chicago to-day and place on my bill and I will arrange special discount. Leave here Monday to see Hayden, Chicago." That telegram informed the operatives in Milwaukee that one and three had left for that city. B. also wired the operative at Monica Junction a similar message so that he could board the train and pick up the shadowing.

CHAPTER XVII

DETECTIVE GETS SUSPECT'S PICTURE

Operative B. had succeeded in making two snapshots of Sullivan. The subject was extremely cautious and insisted on having a time exposure picture made when the women of the Steinmetz house insisted on his coming into the group. He protested at first against having any picture made, but he was a "ladies' " man and was susceptible to their pleadings. He thought to satisfy them and also avoid having his features show in the finished group. He fixed the camera of the operative so that it would take a time exposure. By moving his head the fraction of an inch he would blur the picture and hide his features in the negative.

This was a clever enough scheme to fool an amateur, but Operative B. was no amateur. He took the camera from Sullivan and slipped the little lever back to "Instantaneous" and then pretended to be making a time exposure while, in reality, he made two good snapshots.

The operatives had reported daily out of the wilderness and had sent specimens of Sullivan's handwriting. These with the picture and with information we secured at Indianapolis proved to us that we had our man—J. B. Bryce!

Here was the actual murderer of the twenty-one newspaper workers who were sent to their death in the destruction of the Los Angeles Times. We had him but he was better at large than in jail. The time had not come for slipping the handcuffs on him. He would lead us to the man above him, John J. McNamara. He would lead us to the whole crew of "leaders" who engaged in the conspiracy against society and who had turned a big and once powerful labor organization into a band of Anarchists working with notoriously confessed Anarchists of the rankest type.

Our operatives picked up McManigal and the rest of the hunting party as they left the train; to tail them until the final round-up. But each shadow had the instructions to sacrifice anything rather than have the man he was following realize that he was being shadowed.

Sullivan or Bryce was left alone at Conover by the others and the sense of security he had enjoyed because of the presence of friends and fellow criminals began to desert him. He became suspicious of his friend "Billy," Operative B., and suddenly announced that he would leave that very morning, December 5. B. hurried into his traveling clothes and produced his telegram which would warrant him in starting away with the subject. Then Bryce changed his mind and remained in his room at the

Steinmetz house until the train departed. B. might have made a bluff at leaving but he knew that Bryce was friendly with the ticket agent and so he bought a ticket through to Chicago, took the train and hopped off at Milwaukee where he connected with Operative R. J. K. He was fearful that Bryce might take a freight train from Conover and so he waited until the freight pulled into Milwaukee at 2:20 a. m. and assured himself that his man was not on it.

The record of the last day spent by Operative B. and Bryce together in the woods of Wisconsin, when fear began to creep into the heart of the dynamiter, is told graphically by my investigator as follows:

"Operative B. reports:

"Conover, Wis., Mon., Dec. 5th, 1910.

"At 7:20 a. m. No. 2 came over to my shack and remained with me talking about getting a party together to go fishing to-day at Scott Lake, six miles south of Conover. After breakfast he told me he was not feeling well from his jag and wanted to go away from where he could get any booze. Within a half hour, No. 2, Frank Rempert and his assistant Tony, Mary Thomas, Alice and Tillie Steinmetz and I left the town in a hand car for Scott Lake, and just as we were about to start, I got the crowd to pose for a picture, and while I was getting the distance, etc., No. 2 tried several times to hide himself behind the others, and after that while at the Lake whenever anyone suggested taking a picture, I asked No. 2 to take it, which he willingly agreed to do. One time while he and Mary Thomas were several hundred feet out on the lake, he knelt down and let Mary Thomas sit on his knee and I dared him to let me take a picture of him in that attitude; he agreed, providing I would get in the picture, which I did and let Tony, the section hand, take the snap shot. Another time, one of the girls wanted her picture taken and asked No. 2 and the others to get in it and No. 2 hung behind in a suspicious way and insisted that I take a time picture, which I did, but I think he suggested that so as to give him a chance to move and blur his picture.

"While at the lake No. 2 spent most of his time with the girls, but while with me one time said he could have left here with No. 1, that he is working for No. 1, and that he guessed No. 1 had little confidence in him after this last jag. I asked him what was the good of worrying, and he said: 'I'm not worrying now over that; that's all I have done for a month is worry, and I am going to cut it out; it does not get anyone anything; what is done cannot be undone.' He also said that he was very easily worried, and half the time he did not know what he worried about. Several times he remarked that he was sorry he did not go to Chicago with the others yesterday.

"No. 2 was very quiet all day, and only had one drink all day up to four o'clock this afternoon, and was sober and seemed to be giving something much thought. When he would sit with his chin resting on his hands, I remarked for him to come out of the trance he was in, and he said, 'I am sorry that I did not return with No. 1, but I will see him to-morrow night.'

"During the evening he told Henry Steinmetz that No. 1 lived at 414 S. Sangamon Street, Chicago. After our return from the lake, No. 2 ordered several rounds of drinks for the family, and 2 then shaved himself with a safety razor, which he had in his suit case, and put on his brown suit. No. 2 is letting his blond mustache grow, and also side whiskers, and when one of the Steinmetz girls asked why he let them grow he said it was because he had his jaw dislocated. Later, in answer to a similar question from Mrs. Steinmetz, he said the bones showed too plainly. On one corner of his mouth, on the left, is a white mole about this size 'O' and about half inch below his side burner on the left side are two smaller white moles, and on the right of his large Roman nose he has a light brown mole. The upper right eye tooth has a gold crown, and all the rest of his teeth are white and even, especially the lower teeth.

"He is wearing a cheap ready-made light brown suit and light-brown fedora hat, wears no rings, but has a heavy gold watch chain with a locket. His whole make-up is that of a refined farmer. He has no overcoat with him. Has two suit cases; one is a very good leather one (new), while the other is old, and a dark imitation alligator skin."

CHAPTER XVIII

THE MEETING OF THE DYNAMITERS

After his false start for Chicago and the short stay in Milwaukee, Operative B. took a train back for Conover on the afternoon of December 7. Changing cars at Monica Junction he was informed that Sullivan had left Conover for Watersmeat station, where he had taken a through train with Pullman berth for Chicago. Operative B. picked up Operative W. H. C. at Monica Junction and instructed him to wire him in the business code arranged so that he could turn back at Conover and leave for Chicago. He was still covering himself thoroughly, although his man was many miles away. It was good detective work, for he had roped the subject, and it would be his business perhaps to run into him again and maintain that friendship he had created.

B. went on to Conover and the Steinmetz girls told him that after his departure Sullivan had looked over some letters and had said that he had overlooked an important matter, and would have to hurry to Chicago. This was merely an excuse for getting away alone. The girls said that Sullivan

cried when he left the house and that he promised
to write to the family and send the children Christmas presents.

All this time my son Raymond, from his Chicago
office, was having McManigal shadowed day and
night, and his home in Sangamon Street watched by
the pick of his men.

Sullivan, after leaving the train from Conover,
went directly to the home of McManigal with Operative B. F. D. following him. This operative had
known him while he was refugeeing in the woods
and so dared not take the same trolley car he took
from the depot. He jumped into a taxi and had
the chauffeur follow the car.

Sullivan remained only twenty minutes in the
home of McManigal, and then left the house with
him. My son Raymond and Operative A. V. were
also in the vicinity of McManigal's house when the
two subjects connected. It was an important moment in the hunt for the perpetrators of the Los
Angeles crime and the scores of other crimes that
had made the reign of terror in the United States.
Two dynamiters, both murderous, desperate men,
were walking the streets of the second largest city
in the country, passing policemen, courts of justice
and perfectly free of any hindrance from the ordinary machinery of law.

The two men boarded an eastbound Van Buren
street car, and our shadows followed in a taxi to
the Dearborn Street station. They boarded a

Monon train which left at 12.10 p. m., and sat in a forward coach, talking earnestly and in whispers. As the train was about to start McManigal jumped off and one of our shadows took him up again. Sullivan remained on the train and went to Indianapolis. He was going to report to headquarters. Two operatives followed him. He would never again be without a shadow until he was safe in prison.

Operative B. F. D. left the train with him, saw him check one of his grips and take the other with him. Sullivan went one block up Illinois Street and boarded a Pennsylvania Avenue car. Endeavoring to throw off any shadow that might be after him, Sullivan alighted at Market Street and entered the Dennison Hotel. He passed through the hotel and slipped out of a side entrance, and then hurried to the Plaza Hotel. He registered as F. Sullivan, City, and was given Room 179. B. F. D. covered the hotel until one in the morning, when Operative A. V. relieved him for the remainder of the night.

In all probability Sullivan got in touch with headquarters by telephone. He left Indianapolis the next morning for Cincinnati, and on arrival there checked his grip and left the station to seek shelter in a nearby drug store. He was waiting for some one, and would leave the drug store occasionally to cross to the station and look at the train schedule. He bought a ticket for Northside, a suburb of the city, and at 1.35 p. m. a tall, clean-shaven stranger alighted from a train from Indianapolis. The stranger also purchased a ticket for Northside and greeted Sullivan. They took a train for the suburban settlement at 2.45 p. m. The stranger carried two packages wrapped in paper and Sullivan two grips.

Arriving at Northside the two subjects separated, the stranger taking a trolley, one of our operatives following him. Sullivan walked to Chase Street to Virginia Street, through an unlighted street and up a hill with a few small houses on it. The neighborhood was very tough, unlighted and without sidewalks. The operatives following Sullivan came to the end of this street, and there was danger of getting too close to the subject. Because of the topography they had no way of covering themselves. They decided to drop their man and return to the station. At the station they found Operative P. J. B., who had tailed the stranger. Comparing notes they found that the two men had gone the same way and to the same place. Our men had to wait until daylight to locate their subjects. They took a car to Cincinnati, and there got a few hours' rest.

We now had three men fully covered, namely; McManigal, known in the reports as Subject 1; Sullivan, known in the reports as Subject 2, and the stranger who connected with Sullivan and who will be referred to as Subject 3.

The reader might think that good luck played a part in the appearance of the stranger, Subject 3,

when he met Sullivan in the Cincinnati station while
Sullivan was under surveillance. But luck had nothing to do with it. Subject 3 brought his own shadow
with him to that meeting, and the shadow had followed him from the headquarters of the International Union of Bridge and Structural Iron Workers in Indianapolis.

In a detective operation as large as the one in-
volving the structural iron workers' strike and the
resulting crimes perpetrated by the men at the head
of the union so many men are used, and there are
so many different ends to the case that frequently
operatives will be working in the same city on the
same case without knowing the nature of each
others task.

When I undertook the work of finding the men
guilty of the Los Angeles crime and putting an end
to the reign of terror my agency had attained such
excellent growth that I was able to direct the work
through my managers in the various parts of the
country, keeping each district separate so that there
would be no waste of energy and effort by one force
running into the field of another. Wherever I
might be, whether among the Anarchists at Home
Colony or in my New York offices or in a hotel
room, I always kept communication established with
my son Raymond in Chicago and with those operatives who were immediately available for quick
work that circumstances might demand.

In frequent journeys across the continent I could

be reached by telegraph wherever the train might pause and my managers could tell in a moment just what part of the country my train was speeding through. Every operative reported every day by wire, and then more fully by letter, and through thousands of these reports we studied the progress of the case and marked off clues and trails that had been run out to the end.

As I have said in public addresses, private detective agencies are too frequently the means for blackmailing, and the private detective has all the opportunity in the world to develop into a blackmailer. In assembling my force, which now numbers over 1,200 men, including men of every profession from the college professor to the day laborer, we strove to employ only men we could trust implicitly. I believe that we succeeded in getting as clean a corps of intelligent operatives as has ever been assembled by one man engaged in the profession of detection. Many of them could have sold out on me during the McNamara case, but not one of them yielded to the offers of bribes made them.

This digression is merely to show the reader how far we could and did trust our operatives and how wide was the net we spread for the dynamiters.

As the net was woven stronger with each fresh discovery of our investigators we drew it closer and closer about the big fish in the gigantic conspiracy of wreck and murder and ruin. The expense of maintaining the number of men I did in a nation-wide search was extremely heavy, and at one time I found myself without enough funds from Los Angeles to go on with the investigation. The detective in fiction never has to bother about money, but my men had to be paid, heavy telegraph tolls had to be met with cash payments, thousands of dollars had to be paid in railroad fares and hotel bills and bills for subsistence. I had gone too far to stop, for I was certain of the men who had committed all these crimes, and it was a matter of public safety that these criminals be put where they could not imperil not only the property of the people they were fighting but also the lives of thousands of innocent people who were not at all concerned in the outcome of the strike.

I financed the investigation myself for the time being, and kept my men busy in many parts of the country.

CHAPTER XIX

SHADOWING THE MCNAMARAS AT HOME

When the operatives trailing Sullivan and the tall, clean-shaven stranger came upon the suburb of Northside it was new territory for them. The two men they had under surveillance had passed through Northside to where the country became ragged and broken, and where a clump of houses was known as Cumminsville before that area was taken into the city limits of Cincinnati.

Over a month before their arrival we had sent Operative H. B. M. to Cincinnati with instructions to locate James B. McNamara, brother of J. J. McNamara, secretary-treasurer of the International Union of Bridge and Structural Iron Workers. This operator first looked up a city directory and found James B. McNamara set forth there as a printer, and his residence put down as 4306 Quarry Street. He started out to find this address, and finally located Quarry Street in the old Cumminsville section and the house in the extreme northwest corner of the settlement. It was a hilly section and the street difficult to find. It was short and boasted only four houses, the last house to the north being

No. 4306. It was the most pretentious of the four, being a two-story frame house surrounded by an iron fence set in concrete.

The operative might have a long wait for the return home of James B. McNamara, and so he sought to get a room in the neighborhood. He was unable to get one, and so had to content himself with headquarters in the nearest saloon kept by a man named Fred Haus. He learned that the house was occupied by Mrs. Mary T. McNamara, and that her son James B. spent a good part of his time away from Cincinnati. None of the people in the neighborhood knew what he did for a living. The gossip was that he had a wife in Chicago.

The reader will now see how the net was being drawn in around the principals in the wholesale Los Angeles murder. Three sets of operatives came together at this point in the progress of the case.

Sullivan had two shadows escort him to the home of Mrs. McNamara. The clean-shaven stranger had another shadow see him over the threshold and there was still another shadow awaiting their arrival.

The two visitors to the little house in the little street among the hills of Cumminsville were the two sons of Mrs. McNamara, J. J. and James B.

Subject No. 1, first known as J. W. McGraw, was Ortie McManigal, and we had him well in hand.

Subject No. 2, first known in San Francisco as J. B. Bryce, and then in the woods of Wisconsin as

Frank Sullivan, was James B. McNamara. We had him where we could put the nippers on him at any moment.

Subject No. 3, the clean-shaven man who had connected with James B. McNamara after his return from refugeeing in the Wisconsin woods, was J. J. McNamara. We could always find him when we needed him, and we kept him shadowed constantly.

We had witnesses to identify McGraw as the man who bought the nitroglycerin at Portland, Ind., from Morehart, and we had his sawdust trail to East Peoria, where the McClintic-Marshall girders were blown up.

We had witnesses to identify James B. McNamara as the man who bought the dynamite for the Los Angeles explosion, and we had his signatures as Bryce, as Sullivan and his own signature to connect him up by means of expert testimony in handwriting.

We had no real convincing evidence against J. J. McNamara, who was the directing mind of all the explosions and assaults. Nor had we enough evidence to warrant successful prosecution against Tveitmoe, Hockin, Ryan and the 45 other labor "leaders" who were subsequently indicted by the Federal grand jury in Indianapolis for conspiracy. We were far from the end of the case.

On December 12, 1910, our operatives started the surveillance of the McNamara home wherein were the two men who were to be sent to prison later on their own pleas of guilty to the charge of murder.

For any one in the cottages on Quarry Street to make his way to the station at Northside or the trolley going into Cincinnati it would be necessary to pass the junction of two highways known as Colerain and Virginia Avenues. This was the point where real streets with sidewalks began, where there were more houses, a saloon or two and a shop or two. Between this point and Quarry Street there was no cover for a shadow and our men had a hard time of it watching the McNamara house. A man was always on duty at Colerain and Virginia Avenues.

On the first morning of the surveillance J. J. McNamara left his mother's home and boarded a street car for Cincinnati proper. Operatives A. V. and P. J. B. followed him. The subject alighted at one of the principal corners in the city, Walnut and Sixth Streets. He walked the length of a block twice on the same side of the street, stopping every twenty-five or thirty feet and looking about and scanning the faces of the people near him. It was evident that he wanted to find out whether he was being followed, and my operatives, following the standing instruction never to let a subject uncover a shadow, dropped him and went back to Cumminsville.

The surveillance was kept up night and day. During the daytime the operatives managed to get to the top of a steep hill which overlooked the cottages on Quarry Street. They had a bird's-eye view from there, and soon found cross-country paths they could utilize for quick trips back to the car line. One operative lying in the bushes on this hill had a close call from death. He wore a brown felt hat, just about the color of a rabbit. It was all that showed over the tops of the bushes. He was startled when a hunting dog ran through the brush to him. He turned in time to see a hunter with a shotgun leveled at his head. The operative yelled in time to show the hunter his peril and then rolled over and pretended to sleep.

In the nighttime the operatives could approach the cottages on Quarry Street without risk of being uncovered. But the movements of the subjects after night gave them little chance of discovering anything. They remained indoors and the blinds of the house were generally drawn.

Finally J. J. McNamara was compelled to return to his office in Indianapolis. He did so, and his arrival there was duly reported from an operative who had engaged a room which gave him a good view of the offices of the International Union in the American Central Life Building. This operative wired the Chicago office: "Have three machine." This was to inform Manager Raymond Burns that he had picked up Subject No. 3.

All during the early spring of 1911, J. J. McNa-

mara moved always with a shadow, and his frequent
attempts to catch some one following him failed.
He felt secure, and in that feeling of security went
on with this work of directing his destructive forces.

About Easter time he left Indianapolis headquarters and started for the station. To cover himself,
as he thought, he slipped into a large building and
out by another entrance. The operative shadowing
him knew that in a few minutes a train was due to
leave the Union depot for Cincinnati so he went
there instead of trying to hunt his man in the building. Two operatives were already there watching
all incoming and outgoing trains. He picked up his
man again and followed him to Cincinnati and then
to Cumminsville and his mother's home. The following day the operatives followed J. J. to church
with his mother. That night J. J. eluded our
watchers, but was picked up by the operative at Indianapolis headquarters the next morning, and we
called our Cumminsville men from a cold trail.

From the time of the return of James B. McNamara from hiding in the Wisconsin woods to April
22d, 1911, we followed every step made by the three
subjects, J. J., J. B., and McManigal. We knew
where their explosives were stowed, we knew their
system of planting their bombs and setting them off,
we knew every time F. M. Ryan, the president of
the International Union, and E. A. Clancy and
other labor "leaders" met with J. J. McNamara,
the directing mind of the acts of violence. We had

uncovered the personal and private sides of their lives, and on April 22d we were ready to act.

We had used six months and twenty-two days in the investigation.

Before giving the details of the arrests I shall give an account of the detective work done from the McManigal end of the problem, leading to the arrests of McManigal and James B. McNamara as they went forth at the direction of J. J. McNamara to blow up a number of nonunion plants.

CHAPTER XX

BURNS' MEETING WITH HOCKIN

We were waiting to catch J. J. McNamara in the act of participating in some of the dynamiting schemes. My idea, in order to make this complete, was to catch either Caplan or "Schmidtie," and get a confession from them, and implicate the "higher-ups."

In the meantime, I learned from my son that a Mr. Jewell, connected with the McClintic-Marshall Construction Company, had given us information to the effect that the man who Mr. McClintic had previously informed me was furnishing them with information was Herbert S. Hockin, and that they had arranged to have him communicate with us. I then returned to Chicago, and my son arranged with me for a meeting with Hockin. I met Hockin, and he was extremely nervous, and very reticent. He told me, however, that when he learned from J. J. McNamara that his (McNamara's) purpose was to sacrifice human life for the purpose of bringing about the results he hoped to obtain—whatever they were—that he then made up his mind that he would have nothing whatever to do with that. He feared

132

that his course would result in disaster to organized labor, and feared that to complain within the ranks of organized labor might not have the desired effect. He thereupon called on McClintic-Marshall. After the destruction of the Los Angeles Times, Hockin endeavored to reach me entirely outside of McClintic-Marshall, without consulting with them at all, through another detective agency in Chicago. This, however, was at a time when we had in the hands of McClintic-Marshall, our clients, a report showing that our operative, in his investigation of the Peoria matter, was in Indianapolis, and his investigation further showed that J. J. McNamara and Hockin were the two men upon whom we had placed the responsibility for the Peoria matter. They had been there before the explosion; so my son told me that he had met Hockin and that Hockin had made this statement to him that I have just related.

Hockin insisted, from the very start, that the only man that he knew who was connected with this and also connected with organized labor was J. J. McNamara; that while he suspected Tveitmoe's connection with it, he had no evidence. Now I said to Hockin: "Do you know that we have in the hands of McClintic-Marshall now a report showing that we have carried the Peoria investigation right up to the headquarters of the International Bridge and Structural Iron Workers?" He said "no." He did not know that. And I said to him: "You are coming late in the day, when we are about to grab you and J. J. McNamara." He replied that he did not know that I had that report in the hands of Mc-Clintic-Marshall. I then asked him who J. W. Mc-Graw was, and I gave him a description. He stated that it was Ortie McManigal; that he lived in Chicago; that the other man being used was a brother to J. J. McNamara by the name of J. B. McNamara. And, firmly believing that Hockin's purpose was to eliminate the radical element from organized labor, and that he would work honestly and sincerely with us, because he seemed to be thoroughly honest in his convictions, I then suggested to him that we would pay him for his work and for his trouble. He stated that he wouldn't accept anything; that we couldn't pay him money enough, and that no matter how much money we offered him, it wouldn't tempt him, but what he would accept would be for whatever expenses might be incurred in coming to see me from time to time. I urged him very strongly to make a fuller explanation as to what connection the International had with the matter, and he insisted that they appropriated one thousand dollars a month to J. J. McNamara, and they didn't know what he did with that money. They naturally supposed he was using it for "organization" purposes.

It was after talking with Hockin that I put "long shadows" on McManigal and J. B. McNamara.

I was satisfied that J. J. McNamara, sooner or

later, would personally participate in these dynamitings, and I had in mind all the while that it would
take evidence of the very strongest and most con-
clusive character to convict him, because of the fact
that he was a lawyer and he occupied an important
position—that of secretary and treasurer of the International Union.

In the meantime our men covering McManigal's
house, owing to the great precaution they had to
take, frequently missed McManigal going in and
out, but, on one occasion, found McManigal and
Jim McNamara coming out of the house carrying
two large bundles. They carried them downtown,
and then began a series of tests, which compelled
our men to drop them. The following morning we
read where this dynamite was exploded in South
Chicago, without doing any damage whatever.

Finding that I was having a serious time about
my money at Los Angeles, and by this time having
something over $14,000 invested in the matter, and
knowing that unless I succeeded in actually capturing the men responsible for the blowing up of the
Times I would lose that amount of money, I
made up my mind that I would have to take a
chance on rounding them up, and felt that I might
possibly be able to secure a confession from Ortie
McManigal which would serve in lieu of a confession from "Schmidtie" or Caplan. Being hard
pressed for money at this time, I was compelled to
go to friends and borrow $10,000.

We then began to draw the lines tightly about the McNamaras. We established a closer espionage on J. J. in Indianapolis by securing a place directly opposite the building where the office of the McNamaras was located, and we also secured a place across the street from the building in which Ortie McManigal's apartment was located.

CHAPTER XXI

BRIBES OFFERED AT TIME OF ARRESTS

We were all ready for the arrests when McManigal packed his grip in the Sangamon Street flat and kissed his wife and children good-by. We were waiting for him to join J. B. McNamara and start with him on their next round of destruction.

Operative McL. was to keep on the heels of Subject No. 1, McManigal. Subject No. 2, J. B. Mc-Namara, was already well shadowed, and I was waiting for the right moment to walk into the headquarters of the International Union and make a prisoner of J. J. McNamara.

On the morning of April 11 McManigal made his start to join Jim McNamara. Here is the running report of Operative McL. from seven o'clock in the morning of that date until 7.30 in the evening of April 15th.

Operative McL. reports:

"At 7 a. m. I arrived at place of cover opposite Subject No. 1's home. During the morning nothing was seen of Subject No. 1. At 12.30 p. m. I left for lunch, leaving A. V. to cover the house.

I returned at 1.20 p. m. and found A. V. gone. I
immediately telephoned the agency and learned that
A. V. and B. F. D. were at the La Salle depot with
No. 1, who was about to leave on Lake Shore train.
I proceeded to the depot and boarded Lake Shore
train as it was pulling out at 1.40 p. m. and joined
A. V. and B. F. D. in the second coach from rear.
I saw Subject No. 1 in the coach. He sat on the left
side of car, about the seventh seat from the rear.
He had a suit case on the floor at his feet, which
he guarded very closely and did not leave his seat
once until the train arrived in Toledo, O., at 7.40
p. m. Leaving the train with the suit case, he entered the waiting room of the depot, where he was
met by Subject No. 2, who, apparently, was waiting
for him. They shook hands and stood talking for
a moment, then Subject No. 1 sat down on a bench
and unfolded a map which they looked at. Subject
No. 1, with a lead pencil, was designating places on
the map to No. 2, who was standing in front of him.
About ten minutes later, No. 1 and No. 2 left the
depot and walked up the street to the Meyerhof
Hotel, where they registered and were assigned to
room No. 11. Subject registered as G. Foster,
Cleveland. I did not have time to observe how No.
2 had registered. Leaving A. V. and B. F. D. to
cover the hotel, I went to the Union Depot, and
telephoned Manager R. J. B. at Chicago, and told
him we had Subjects No. 1 and No. 2 under surveillance. R. J. B. instructed me to keep them under

surveillance; that he would get officers and leave on
the first train for Toledo. During the evening, the
subjects went to a show and returned to the Meyerhof Hotel at 11.10 p. m.

"On the morning of April 12 at 4.45 a. m. I met
Manager R. J. B. with the detectives, as they arrived at the Union Depot, Toledo. We proceeded
to a hotel just this side of the Meyerhof and from a
room on the third floor covered the entrance to the
Meyerhof Hotel. A. V. and B. F. D. were in a
room farther up the street. All exits from the
Meyerhof were covered, and there was no chance
for them to leave unobserved. About 8.45 a. m.
we observed subjects in the lobby of the Meyerhof.
They sat in rockers at the window, apparently engaged in earnest conversation. About 10 a. m.
they left the hotel and started toward the Union
Depot. No. 1 carried suit case. Arriving at the
Union Depot, Subject No. 1 got in line at the ticket
window and purchased two tickets to Detroit.
While No. 1 was buying the tickets, No. 2 was getting a grip at the news stand, which evidently he
had checked there the day before. Subjects boarded
train which left Toledo at 10.30 a. m., arriving in
Detroit at 12.25 p. m. Subjects carried their re-
spective grips, walked up the street, and finally entered the Oxford Hotel, and registered, No. 1 as
G. Foster, Cleveland, and No. 2 as F. Caldwell,
Cleveland.

"While subjects were still in this hotel, it was de-

cided not to wait any longer in making the arrest.
Possibly ten minutes after subjects had entered the
Oxford Hotel, registered and checked their grips
and were about to leave, we made the arrest, Manager R. J. B. and Detective Sergeant Biddinger,
No. 1, and Detective Sergeant Reed and I taking
No. 2 into custody. Subjects were taken to the
depot, our intentions being to bring them on to Chicago. Subject No. 2 objected, and demanded that
he be taken to Police Headquarters, which was
done. No. 1 was willing to return, and he finally
prevailed on No. 2 to sign a waiver and come to
Chicago. Subjects had given us the checks to their
grips at the Oxford Hotel. The grips were taken
to the Cadillac Hotel, Room 275, and there opened
in the presence of the Detroit police officers, and
the contents examined. The grips contained clocks
attached to batteries, fuses, wire, two magazine
guns, one rifle with sound muffler, small kit of tools,
camera and numerous other articles. About 11.15
p. m. we left Detroit with the subjects. Subjects
wanted to know what they were arrested for. We
told them they were wanted for safe blowing.

"En route Detroit to Chicago, Subject No. 2 became very talkative. He said: 'You fellows don't
want me for safe blowing. Why, I never cracked a
safe in my life. You men are making a mistake. I
have got the American Federation of Labor behind
me with hundreds of thousands of dollars. I am
another Vincent Altman. They didn't convict him,

did they? Well, they will never convict me if they take me back to that scabby ——— town in California.' At one time, with his hands clenched and trembling from head to foot, he said: 'I know you have got the goods on me. I am going to die; yes, I am going to die, but I will die a martyr to Unionism and Socialism.' He kept repeating: 'They didn't convict Altman, and you can never get 12 men to convict me.' Finally he said: 'You men have a price. How much do you want?' He offered us $10,000, then $20,000, then $30,000 if we would take him and his partner off the train before we got into Chicago and give him 36 hours to reach his friends. He called them 'The men upstairs' or 'The men higher up.' All this, and we had never said one word to them as to the real cause of their arrest.

"At one time he said with great emotion: 'If you take me to Chicago it will be too late (meaning to give us the bribe money to let them go). There is only one man in Chicago I am afraid of, and that is W. J. Burns.' "

The two men were arrested under their aliases, and they were given to understand that they were wanted as yeggmen. We had not yet shown our hand, and were not ready to put it on the table in the game until we had Subjects 1, 2 and 3 safely in prison in Los Angeles.

In arresting McManigal, Operative McL. used

his knowledge of events gained in shadowing him to good advantage. McManigal turned on him and said: "You don't know anything about me."

"Why, I even know where you bought the shoes you've got on," was the quiet reply of the operative.

McManigal laughed and asked him where he had bought them.

"At No. 117 State Street, Chicago," said the operative. "They are Walkover shoes, and you bought them on the evening of April 8."

McManigal was astonished as he realized that he had been under the closest kind of surveillance and some of his confidence was shaken.

"I can even tell you what your wife dreamed the night before you left home," added McL.

McManigal looked at him as if to challenge the assertion.

"She dreamed that the police were after you, and that you had drawn your pistol, and that you had shot yourself," McL. told him.

Mrs. McManigal had told her husband this just before he left home, and, although it may puzzle the reader to figure out just how McL. learned of this, it was simply enough done. Mrs. McManigal had been in the habit of consulting a fortune teller. The shadow had consulted her also. The fortune teller had known of the mysterious way of McManigal's livelihood, and had taken a chance on the story of the police and McManigal. Mrs. McManigal, not wanting her husband to know that she con-

sulted fortune tellers, told him that she had dreamed
this thing.

McManigal was quick to realize that he was terribly tight in the grip of the law. He was not slow
to appreciate the fact that Jim McNamara would
have behind him all the influence his brother could
command from the union forces, and he saw himself
in a position where the blame for the whole five
years of crime would be put his way. His only
chance of saving his life was to turn State's evidence. McManigal is nobody's fool. He thought
of the chances of saving his own neck, and he
thought at the same time of his wife and children.
He had been the tool of J. J. McNamara and the
men who conspired with him in the masked war,
just as Schmidt and Caplan, the two Anarchists, had
been used as tools.

From the daily reports of the operatives shadowing McManigal I had a pretty good idea of the
make-up of the man both as a dynamiter and as husband and father. As long as I had him safely away
from the influence of J. J. McNamara and the lawyers of the union I could hope to exert upon him an
influence that would show him the advantage of telling the truth and the whole truth. A confession
from McManigal would mean conviction of the Mc-
Namaras and the drawing into the net, for trial on
conspiracy charges, Ryan, the president of the International, Hockin, Tveitmoe, Munsey, and the forty
and more others who were J. J. McNamara's aides

in the waging of the war with torch and dynamite and nitroglycerin.

My son Raymond, who directed the arrests of Jim McNamara and McManigal, had taken the two men prisoner at exactly the right moment. The plans they had studied together on meeting in Toledo were plans showing nonunion jobs in Detroit which they had been sent out to cripple or destroy. Their grips were filled with the paraphernalia of their mode of warfare. Here is the short report of my son Raymond in which he gives the list of things found in the bags of the two prisoners.

Manager Raymond J. Burns reports:

At 8 p. m. on the night of April 11th, 1911, Operative McLaren called me on long-distance phone from Toledo, O., and stated that McManigal had connected with J. B. McNamara at Toledo. I immediately got in touch with Sergeants Reed and Biddinger of the Chicago Police Department, and at 11.30 p. m. we left for Toledo, O., via Lake Shore Railroad. I was met at the depot in Toledo by Operative McLaren. We proceeded to the Park Hotel, which is opposite the Meyerhof Hotel, where the two subjects were stopping, and watched the entrance of the Meyerhof from a room on the third floor in the Park Hotel. The next morning we observed the subjects sitting in the lobby of the Meyerhof, where they remained until 10 a. m., then going to the depot and boarding a train for Detroit, which

train Sergeants Reed and Biddinger, Operatives Mc-
Laren and Velton and I also boarded. On arrival
in Detroit, the subjects proceeded to the Oxford
Hotel, where they registered, McNamara registering as F. Caldwell, Cleveland, and McManigal as
G. Foster, Cleveland. They then checked their suit
case and valise. Just as they were leaving the hotel,
they were arrested by Sergeants Reed and Biddinger, assisted by Operative McLaren and myself.
We went to the Union Station, but owing to Mc-
Namara's protestations, he claiming we were kidnapping them, we took the prisoners to the police
station, where they were searched by Lieutenant
John J. Downey and Sergeant Edward Fox of the
Detroit Police Department. We then proceeded to
the Cadillac Hotel, secured the grips of the prisoners in the meantime, and at the aforesaid hotel,
Downey and Fox opened the suit case and valise of
the prisoners with keys which had been taken from
them when they were searched at the police station.
In the suit case were found:

1 Winchester rifle, .22 caliber, No. 125,957,
with Maxim silencer attached.

1 automatic .38-caliber magazine gun, No.
32,998.

1 Eastman Kodak, size 3.

1 camera tripod.

1 ammeter, No. 1002.

1 small size intermittent alarm clock.

1 ball of twine.

1 kit of small tools.

1 box of .38 caliber cartridges.

1 roll of battery wire.

1 roll of bandage.

1 part box of .38 caliber cartridges.

Shirts, collars, ties, stockings, handkerchiefs and pair of shoes.

In the valise were found two dry batteries attached to two small-sized intermittent alarm clocks, also

3 small size intermittent alarm clocks.

1 magazine .32 caliber automatic gun, No. 30,760.

1 roll copper wire.

4 fuse cups.

4 rolls of insulated copper wire, with caps attached.

1 plain board, to which was attached small intermittent alarm clock.

1 roll of fuse.

A number of the above articles were marked for identification at the time they were first examined by Downey as follows: "J. B. D. 2-14-1911."

After getting the two prisoners to sign waivers to return to Chicago, Raymond, McLaren, Velton and Detective Sergeants Reed and Biddinger of Chicago took their men to the Michigan Central train and left with them at 11.24 p. m.

Arriving in Chicago, we arranged so that we would not have to waste time in fighting habeas corpus proceedings and other obstacles that might be thrown in our way by representatives of the dynamiters. We took the prisoners to the home of Sergeant Reed and kept them there pending the arrival of extradition papers. This hiding away of the two men resulted in a long and bitter howl of protest from thousands of labor people who may have believed that the McNamaras were innocent. The indictment for kidnapping brought against me later came to nothing, of course, for there was no kidnapping. We had warrants for the arrest of the men, and all the time they were in custody of Chicago detectives in the home of one of them.

Having Jim McNamara and McManigal safely tucked away in a corner of Chicago's suburbs we then began to arrange for quick extradition to Los Angeles. We wanted extradition papers for three men, for we were ready to walk into the office of the International Union in Indianapolis and take the secretary-treasurer from his desk that he might face the law and answer for his big share in the years of ruthless murder and destruction.

CHAPTER XXII

McMANIGAL DECIDES TO CONFESS

With the two prisoners hidden away in Reed's house in Chicago, and with every man in the capturing party bound to secrecy, there remained three vastly important things to be accomplished. One was the securing of the confession of McManigal. Another matter of big importance was the task of keeping secret in Los Angeles the fact of the arrests until we had our prisoners safely in jail there. The third matter was the arrest of J. J. McNamara and his speedy extradition so that we could begin the journey to the Coast with the three men and without fear of being tied up by legal proceedings in any of the States we would pass through.

I devised a plan for bringing this about, and laid out such a devious journey from Indianapolis and Chicago to the Coast that I felt sure the foxiest of lawyers would not be able to catch up with us.

To get things started quickly in Los Angeles we wired from our Chicago office on the day of our arrival from Detroit with the two prisoners this message:

"We have under arrest and hidden away here Bryce and John Doe, who did Llewellyn job. Have police department proceed immediately to Sacramento, get requisition papers on Illinois, and come here quick as possible. We won't let arrest be known here until officers arrive with papers or they would spend hundred thousand dollars on habeas corpus proceedings, and all sorts of trouble; they offered us $30,000 to release them. We want to send back two of our men and two Chicago department men with the two men you will send. It is of utmost importance you carry out this exactly as I suggest. Keep me posted."

The Chicago office followed this with another telegram to the Los Angeles office, telling the manager to get his chief aides about him to receive further details in our code, the same to be held in strictest confidence. In the translation of this message "B." stands for Bryce, one of Jim McNamara's aliases, and "M." represents McManigal. The message follows:

"Captured with B. and M. twelve clock devices exactly as that found at Los Angeles, all complete with fuse attached. M. states he has been working with B. under direction of secretary named above; was present in June, 1910, when secretary gave final instructions to B., when he left for Coast. M. accompanied him far as Chicago from Indianapolis.

B. told M. they were going make big clean-up at Los Angeles, that there was plenty of money put up. After B. reached Coast secretary told M. he received letter from B. from Frisco in which B. said: 'It now reads Times for News; it will read news for the Times.' When M. read of Los Angeles matter he went to Indianapolis to see secretary. Latter said: '——— ———, see what those fellows are doing out there!' M. said: 'I wonder if that is our fellow.' Secretary replied: 'It was the Times they wanted and got; by God! that ought to make them come across.' Secretary then directed M. not to come to his office too much, was badly frightened and was very nervous. He directed M. to return to Chicago and keep under cover. When B. returned to Chicago from Coast secretary had M. take B. hunting in Wisconsin. There B. told M. all details of Los Angeles matter, also told M. he reported at Frisco to Tveitmoe and he introduced B. to other two fugitives. Later T. attended convention at St. Louis, met secretary, and told him send wreckers back to get Times auxiliary plant, Baker and Llewellyn iron works for Christmas present. Secretary then directed M. to proceed to Los Angeles. He carried with him twelve quarts of stuff, ten-quart can and two quarts in valise. This was furnished him by secretary, also money for trip. On arrival he investigated places, but was afraid to carry out program, and only did what you know of, then went to Frisco, met Clancy of Frisco Iron

Workers Union, and told him to tell T. Christmas present had been delivered. If this is sufficient information wire, and, for God's sake, don't let a word leak out until officers land here with papers. It looks good."

This was sufficient information to get the warrants and requisition papers for the two men arrested and for J. J. McNamara, whom I was soon to arrest in his office in Indianapolis.

Then came the long wait for the arrival of the sheriff, police officers and a representative of the Los Angeles District Attorney. For a little over a week we kept our two prisoners in Detective Sergeant Reed's house, and the Detroit explosions that the crowd at Indianapolis headquarters were waiting and listening for never came off.

The right moment to arrest J. J. McNamara would be when the Los Angeles officers and the requisition papers were at hand. I waited, and, in the meanwhile, talked with McManigal, whose confession was to put in our hands a mass of information of the most astounding sort, every bit of which could be and was amply verified.

McManigal is a man of medium height, rather dark complexioned, powerfully built and a type of citizen most men would hesitate to anger. His forehead is deeply indented, and carries a heavy, ragged scar made by a fall he had when a boy. He is pleasant in his address, and his English is good, although he never got beyond the public schools and always traveled with uneducated people.

Preying on his mind all the time was the thought of his wife and children and their fate. He was genuinely disturbed about them, and had he been a single man I doubt whether he would have made the confession.

I repaired to the home of Sergeant William Reed, and when I entered the room where J. B. McNamara was sitting, I said to him, as I have always said to every man who has ever been taken into custody and with whom I have had anything to do, that I wanted to notify him of his rights. I had previously notified our men not to discuss the case with J. B. McNamara or McManigal until my arrival. I notified J. B. McNamara of his rights, and stated: "I am not an officer of any kind—merely a private detective; I suppose you know who I am?" I then told him my name. He promptly stated that he knew all about me, and knew I was on the level, and that I had that reputation; that he appreciated the warning I had given him. I further added: "We expect to put you on trial for murder in the first degree, and try you for that, and it would not be fair to attempt to get a confession or any incriminating statements from you, and I have issued positive instructions that the men here present with you, and who have you under guard, shall not discuss your case with you, or discuss any phase of it."

I then entered the room where Ortie McManigal

was confined, and warned him of his rights in the
same way, but I immediately laid before McManigal all the facts in our possession and detailed his
movements from time to time, and McManigal was
utterly astounded and dumfounded, and especially
when I told him that the men he met in the Wisconsin woods on his hunting expedition were Burns detectives.   Not only that, he was greatly disturbed
when I informed him that we had his house under
surveillance for a number of months.   I also detailed his movements on the occasion when he and
J. B. McNamara carried the two bundles of dynamite to a place in Chicago, and which was subsequently exploded at that point.   I also detailed a
number of features at Indianapolis which indicated
to him that there was not a move made by him that
we were not thoroughly conversant with.   I was
able to conjecture perfectly his movements which
we had not covered, but which I was enabled to determine from a study of the case.

Finally, as a last and telling stroke, I said to him:
"Perhaps you feel that because you did not accompany J. B. McNamara to Los Angeles on the occasion of his blowing up the Times that you are in no
way responsible for his act?   On the other hand,
when I explain the law of conspiracy you will find
that you were equally as responsible, though you
were not there at the time."   I then explained that
he, J. J. McNamara and J. B. McNamara and
others were engaged in a conspiracy to destroy life

and property, with a view of bringing about certain results; that, in furtherance of that project, he and J. B. McNamara had many, many times caused explosions which resulted in the destruction of property. I then closed by stating that if, after listening to the evidence which we proposed to submit against him, he felt that he wanted to right the wrong he had committed, in so far as he was then able, and if he desired to show a disposition to lead a different life, that I would be glad to hear his statement, but that I wanted it distinctly understood he must do so without any promises of reward or immunity; that even if I were so disposed, I had no power whatever to make any such promises, and that he must take his chances.

I was greatly impressed with the attitude of McManigal, as there was indicated in his every act a thorough earnestness in wanting to aid the prosecution and right the wrong he had done so far as he was able. He said that he would be perfectly willing to make a full confession, and aid us in every way he possibly could. And be it said, to the everlasting credit of Ortie McManigal, that he more than made good, for if ever a human being was crucified, and if ever an effort was made, through the most audacious and murderous methods, it was made by those who were concerned in this wholesale murder, and who are willing to take every chance to turn McManigal back or else still his voice forever!

After making these statements to McManigal, I then said to him: "Now, don't answer me offhand, but think it over. It's a serious matter and will *be* a serious matter to you. So think it over carefully from every viewpoint, and if you have an attorney who is a friend of yours, and who would advise you wholly in your own interest, I would be glad to send for him. In the meantime, if you care to see me let me know." I then left him and returned to my office in Chicago. On my reaching the office I was notified that word had been telephoned in that Mc-Manigal was asking for me. I sent out word to tell him that I would be there. Within an hour another telephone message came, saying: "McManigal wants to see you, and it is very urgent."

"Tell him I will be there," I replied. Within another hour another message came, until about four of those messages were received, and then I repaired to the home of Detective Sergeant Reed, and I found McManigal in an extremely receptive mood.

My purpose in delaying my visit was to permit him to reach that frame of mind where he would not halt when he reached the high places of his confession, but would tell it all, which he did. I had my stenographer take it and write it out, and I then sent for a notary public, and he signed it and swore to it.

CHAPTER XXIII

MCMANIGAL'S START AS A DYNAMITER

After saying that he was thirty-seven years old and that he was born in Bloomville, O., near the town of Tiffin, McManigal swore that he served in the Spanish War with an Ohio regiment. After being mustered out he worked in stone quarries and there got his experience in handling explosives. He finally joined the Structural Iron Workers, and work being slack left his family in Chicago while he hunted a job in Detroit.

McManigal's confession follows:

"While I was at Detroit, I was first spoken to relative to the wrecking matters. I had a talk with the local executive board at Detroit, the members of which were two men whose names I don't know, and H. S. Hockin. Hockin seemed to be the spokesman. He asked me to blow up a job at Detroit—an office building—being erected by a local firm in Detroit—a nonunion job. They agreed at this time to give me $75. Arrangements for this job were all made in the local hall, and dynamite was the explosive used. Hockin told me to go to a stone quarry along the river in Detroit, but we were unable to secure the dynamite there. I knew of a quarry at Bloomville, Ohio, went down there alone, and bought the dynamite of the man in charge of the stone quarry, which was the E. H. France & Son quarry. I purchased thirty pounds; the man did not ask me what I wanted it for nor did I volunteer to tell him. I returned to Detroit and exploded it with a fuse one night. During this time I continued working on the Oscar Daniels job in Detroit. I never went back to see the results of this explosion. All the members of the local executive board were present and participated in the arrangements for these explosions.

"I next went to Clinton, Iowa, where I did a job. Hockin got me to do this. He was then a member of the Executive Board of the International Bridge and Structural Iron Workers' Union. He was known as 'The Organizer.' On this job I was given the double cross by Hockin, as I afterward learned. It appears that there was a certain amount set aside to do this work by the Executive Board of the International Bridge and Structural Iron Workers. I blew up the derrick car, using dynamite which I procured at Ohio. I did this job alone. I exploded it with a fuse. I found out that Hockin held back part of the money due me for this job. Just prior to this, I was acting as foreman of the J. T. Ryerson plant, in the employment of Charles Volkman & Co. Hockin came and took me off this job. Volkman's office was at 122 Dearborn Street, room 22. This was about the spring of 1907.

"There was quite a lapse between this job at Clinton, and the next one I did, which was at Buffalo, N. Y., a railroad bridge which spanned some other railroad tracks. This also was engineered by Hockin. I was supposed to get $200 and expenses, but was only paid $125 and expenses. I demurred to doing this for such a small sum. I did this job alone.

"On my second trip to Bloomville, Ohio, I purchased 100 pounds of dynamite, taking it to Chicago and hiding it in a lot near where I now live.

"Hockin met me in Buffalo the day before the job was pulled off there, and we looked same over, and he suggested how I should do it. In the meantime, it must be understood that while I was doing this work, I continued at my legitimate work.

"I first met J. J. McNamara when I went from Detroit to Indianapolis to go to work on the Pavilion there at the State Fair Grounds. I was still under instructions of Hockin and carried on these jobs leading up to the Buffalo job. I worked for a while at North Evanston on a job putting in foundations for the National Construction Co., under the subcontract of Charles Volkman & Co. During that time Hockin paid me a visit. He said: 'If I send you a man up here with some soup (meaning dynamite) could you use it?' I said: 'I don't know.' I continued: 'But I would throw it into the concrete and let become of it what would.' However, Hockin never sent it.

"About this time I got connected up with a couple of fellows named Jim Hill and Warneke. I think the latter was a teamster. He wore a teamster's button on his coat. I had known Hill for some time previous to this. I was arrested, charged with participating in the theft of some tools which Hill and Warneke stole. After serving 11 days of a 30-day sentence, I was turned loose again in June, 1910.

"I then started to work for J. P. Costello of Chicago, steel erectors, and while working for this firm Hockin paid several visits to my house. He sent J. B. McNamara to my house on a job I was working on at Madison near Western Avenue. I had met this fellow previously at Muncie, Indiana. I was introduced to him by Hockin.

"While here, Hockin purchased some nitroglycerin—180 quarts—out in the country, of some fellow who drove up and met him there with a wagon, and the stuff was changed in boxes from the seller's wagon to one Hockin had. This exchange was made in the country near Muncie, Indiana, it being delivered in a regular nitroglycerin wagon. Hockin made all arrangements for this purchase. We met this wagon five or six miles from Muncie, in a northeast direction. Hockin paid for this. I took it to Muncie and stored it in a house there on an off street, which Hockin had sent me to rent for this purpose.   I paid the rent to the proprietor of this house, but don't know his name.   He had a real estate office there, and is a prominent real estate man.   The rent was paid up until March, 1909, $7 per month, for a period of five months.   This all happened before I went to jail in Chicago.   While in jail awaiting trial, I was told by J. B. McNamara that he carried 64 quarts of the stuff to Rochester, Pa.   (I am not sure this is the name of the place the nitroglycerin was taken.)   It was buried there under an old building and cooper shop.

"In the meantime I was released on bond and started to work for Costello again.   While working for him at Madison and near Western Avenue, Hockin came to me and said he was sending a man to me with a new invention and he would show me how to use it.   J. B. McNamara called on me while I was working at Madison and near Western Avenue, and told me he would call at my house that evening and explain things to me.   He called alone and showed me the machine.   This was a clock and battery arranged apparatus on a board, connected together so that it would form a circuit by soldering the piece of copper on the key to the alarm of the clock.   He told me to set it at any hour and raise the lever and then connect the wires, he having indicated places by marks, and that by putting the cap in this way it would, at the proper hour, when the alarm would go off, come down, make a connection, form a circuit, make a spark, and cause the explo-

sion. Hockin told me this was a new invention, and
J. B. McNamara said he invented it himself.

"I received a telegram from Hockin instructing
me to meet him at Indianapolis on a Saturday at
3.00 p. m., but being delayed, I did not arrive until
12 midnight. I met him at the Lorraine Hotel,
and also met J. J. McNamara there. We went to
McNamara's office, and when we sat down, Hockin
said: 'We have a job we want you to do at Mt.
Vernon, Ill. It is a hoisting car belonging to Mc-
Clintic-Marshall Co.' He said he wanted that
blown up, also another hoisting engine in the yard.
At this time, McClintic-Marshall was constructing
something there (I don't remember what it was);
it was a new building of some sort. Nothing was
said about what I was to be paid, except that Hockin
advanced me $25 for expenses. Hockin arranged a
train schedule for me, same being to go from Indianapolis to St. Louis, then back to Mt. Vernon,
Ill., then by way of Evanston into Chicago. He
had the stuff in a suit case in Indianapolis. There
were two four-quart cans, two clocks and everything
arranged and made up. The cans were packed in
sawdust, and there was some paper put in the suit
case to keep the sawdust from coming out.

CHAPTER XXIV

MCMANIGAL CHEATED ON PAY ROLL

All this time J. J. McNamara was drawing $200 checks in payment for each explosion, and Hockin was holding back $75 on each, grafting both on the union and the hired dynamiter. McManigal tells how he found out that he was being double-crossed. His confession continues:

"I went to Mt. Vernon as per the arranged schedule and found there was a watchman on the job. I tried for two nights to coax him away, but he did not seem anxious to come away. I decided that by causing some excitement in the lower yards, he would get off the cars to investigate, and while he was gone, the other one would go off there. Hockin suggested that I carry this second charge, so as to set it off at some distance from the car, which would attract the watchman's attention. He knew the watchman was there. He instructed me first to endeavor to get the watchman to go away, and if I could not do that to set the first one off at some distance. I set off the first charge in the lower part of the railroad yard under a hoisting engine

belonging to the McClintic-Marshall Co., I think.
I then set the second charge in a suit case under the
other car. I set the clocks for the hoisting engine
to go off first. As I expected, the watchman left
the car, went to investigate, and while he was gone,
the second explosion occurred. I arranged it so that
they would go off about five minutes apart. I then
returned to Chicago, Hockin subsequently met me
at my home in Chicago and paid me $125. J. B.
McNamara was at my house and present at the time
Hockin called and paid me, but McNamara did not
see Hockin pay me, as the latter took me out in the
kitchen and there gave me the money. No one was
at home but we three.

"I then served my jail sentence, and immediately
after reaching home on my release, I received a
wire from Hockin instructing me to meet him at
Cincinnati, calling at the post office, where I would
receive a letter at the general delivery, which would
say just where to meet him. I called as directed,
received the letter, and it said for me to meet him at
the corner of the post office there at such and such
a time, which I did. I also met J. B. McNamara
with him. They boarded a street car and rode
somewhere in the suburbs, where we lay under some
shade trees and discussed the work to be done.
Hockin directed us both to go to Indianapolis, and
get some nitroglycerin and clocks which J. B. Mc-
Namara had already prepared. I remained over
night in Cincinnati at the McAvoy Hotel (I think

that was the name oí the hotel). It is in the business section of the town. McNamara went home. I may have registered there under my own name. I met J. B. McNamara the next morning at the Grand Central station, and we took the Big Four train to Indianapolis. En route, the conversation drifted from one thing to another—the work we were engaged upon, and so forth. We had instructions to go to Cleveland, Ohio, which instructions we had received from Hockin at Cincinnati. His instructions were as follows: 'Go back to Indianapolis and from there to Cleveland, Ohio, taking with you the nitroglycerin and clocks,' which J. B. McNamara had already prepared.

"During the conversation en route, J. B. McNamara said, 'That will be two apiece.' I said, 'What do you mean?' He said, 'Two hundred.' I said, 'No.' He said, 'Why isn't it? Two for you and two for me.' 'On the same job?' I asked. He answered, 'Yes, certainly.' I said, 'Do you mean to tell me that you get $200 for every job you do?' 'Why, certainly,' he said, 'and expenses.' I later ascertained that he was getting his money from J. J. McNamara because he (J. B. McNamara) was on the inside and knew what was being set aside for that purpose. It was being set aside by the Executive Board. J. B. McNamara then said, 'Don't you get that?' I said, 'No; I only get $125 and expenses.' He said, 'You got $200 for the Mt. Vernon job, didn't you?' I said, 'No; I did not.'

We argued about this a moment, and he said, 'Yes, because I seen the stub, and it called for $235.' I said, 'No; you were up at the house when that fellow paid me, and he gave me $125 there and my expenses were $25, which made $150.' He said, 'I thought there was something wrong when he called you in the kitchen and handed you the money. You have been double-crossed.' I said to him, 'I'm not going any further; I'm done.' This was en route from Cincinnati to Indianapolis. On arrival in Indianapolis, we went to the office of J. J. McNamara, where we had two valises which had been packed. We arrived there during the afternoon about 3 o'clock, and found J. J. McNamara in his office. J. B. McNamara said to me on the train, 'You leave it to me—I will tell that fellow' (meaning of course his brother). When we arrived at the office, he took up the matter with J. J. McNamara, saying, 'This fellow has been double-crossed (meaning me) and is pretty damn sore about it. He claims he has $475 due him.' J. J. McNamara asked for an explanation, which I gave him. I explained I only got $125 for the Mt. Vernon job. He looked it up and found a stub for $235, the check being made out in his own name for $235. He then showed me the stubs for each of the cases, all running from $200 up. He said, 'By God! This thing will never be carried on like this.' I said, 'I got to have just as much money as the next man, or there will be nothing stirring.' He told me to go ahead, and he would take care of my affairs. With this assurance from J. J. McNamara, I concluded to go ahead with the work. J. B. McNamara and I proceeded to Cleveland via Big Four R. R. We arrived in Cleveland about midnight or one o'clock in the morning, and went to some hotel, about two blocks from the depot, right across the street from a fire department house. We both registered there; I don't remember the names; remained that night and the next day we located the job 'way up along the valley; some viaduct job of the McClintic-Marshall Co. We arrived there during the forenoon and found it was pretty well guarded. We noticed a number of shanties which were probably used by watchmen, and that night returned with our valises and located nine or ten watchmen. I told J. B. Mc-Namara it looked like suicide to me. The following night we carried the stuff out there, taking four cans wrapped up in paper, and he arranged the setting of the clocks, putting all the stuff together under one pile, and the clocks together. In order to get to the place where he wished to set it, we had to pass by buildings where there were watchmen, but we succeeded in getting by and in getting to the place where J. B. McNamara concluded to set the explosive. He put them all together, so that if one missed, the other would hit. We then got away, and the explosion took place a couple of hours later. I went to the depot and boarded a train for Toledo, stopping at the Park Hotel, where I registered under my correct name. I read of the explosion the next morning in the papers.

"When leaving Cincinnati, Hockin told me he would be in Toledo at the St. Claire Hotel and said for me to come there and call for him, which I did. I had been instructed by J. J. McNamara not to mention anything to Hockin about this double-crossing business until he took the matter up with him. I went to the hotel, and he made arrangements to meet me at the Terminal Station at a certain time. He gave me $100 there, and told me we (meaning J. B. McNamara and myself) should go to Detroit and look over the new depot and tunnels. We did as directed, and looked over the work, but I did not like it, because I was afraid we could not accomplish what Hockin wanted us to do, viz.: put a load of dynamite under any of the derrick cars. I was satisfied that this could not be done, because there would be too many watchmen there. J. B. McNamara went to the post office and received a letter instructing him to send the Chicago man back to Chicago and wait further orders, and he should return to Indianapolis. It must have been that J. J. McNamara had taken the matter of the double-crossing up with Hockin. When he finished reading the letter, I went to Indianapolis, and subsequently J. B. McNamara told me he left the following day. The explosion at Cleveland took place on June 21st, 1910. On June 27th, 1910, I received $100 from Hockin at Toledo, Ohio.

"On July 8, 1910, I blew the Phœnix Bridge Co. work of Jersey City, N. J. I did this work alone. J. J. McNamara sent me there. On this occasion I received my first money from J. J. McNamara— $200, and my expenses. He paid me at his office in Indianapolis, and said: 'There'll be no double-crossing or holding out by me. What you are entitled to you will get.'

"Between June 27th and July 8th, 1910, I received a telegram at Chicago from J. J. McNamara (I don't think it was signed by that name, but I knew it was from him, as I had an understanding with him, previously arranged at Indianapolis, that any time I received a telegram from Indianapolis I should know it was from him and should destroy it at once to leave no evidence). I received instructions to go to New York, at which time he gave me the nitroglycerin in a suit case all ready to be set off except connecting the clock. J. J. McNamara instructed me to stop off at Pittsburg and make an investigation as to what was doing there in the way of building.

"I want to make a correction at this time, viz.: I did not go to Chicago from Detroit, but instead I went to Pittsburg and there met Hockin again. This visit comes in between June 27th and July 28th, previous to my trip to New York. While there he received a telegram from J. J. McNamara, stating, 'Call all bets off; nothing doing,' meaning by that they should not go ahead with any further work,

and directed Hockin to send me back to Chicago
and for him to return to headquarters. We left together, and on the way back, stopped at Beaver.
Hockin took me over to Rochester, Pa. (I think
that's the place), showed me where this stuff was
buried, and we got three four-quart cans, put them
in a suit case and took them to Cleveland. We were
met at the depot there by two men, whom I had
never seen before, but Hockin knew one and had a
conversation with him, and the other came to me
and said, 'I will relieve you of your load.' He
picked up the suit case and walked away with it. I
do not know what he did with it. I subsequently
learned that it was Nipper Anderson who took this
suit case from me, either through Hockin at the
time or later. I learned the other was Smith or
Schmitty, and he was connected with Local No. 17,
Cleveland. He is a man of about 35 years, 5 feet
8 or 8½ inches, sandy mustache (not sure about
the mustache). I met him since at Cleveland.
Nipper Anderson also belongs there. We were relieved of the suit cases by Schmitty and Anderson. I
then returned to Chicago. I subsequently learned
that it was taken to Akron or Canton, the former I
think, and exploded there under some shops. I saw
an account of it later in the paper.

"On my next trip to Indianapolis, I discussed it
with J. J. McNamara. He asked me whether I
had brought any stuff to Cleveland, and how much.
I then told him about it. McNamara then ar-

ranged for me to go to Jersey City, N. J., which
has already been explained, and pull off the Phœnix
Company job. He furnished me with the suit case,
containing the nitroglycerin and two clocks. As
already stated, I went there and succeeded in getting
it off as desired, for which I received $200 and ex-
penses. On my way back I stopped off at Pittsburg
and found McNamara working on some viaduct
there. On my trip to Jersey City I had three clocks
so that in case one went wrong, I would have another. Since I had no trouble in Jersey City, I had
an extra clock on getting to Pittsburg. I went down
to Rochester and got one four-quart can and took it
up. The first night I did not succeed in getting any
of the work.

"In Pittsburg I stopped at a hotel near the post
office, one block off of Smithfield Street, McGraw.
(This is what gave me the idea of using the name
of McGraw at the places I will subsequently explain.) I went down the next night and got in on
the work and set it off. I had no trouble getting in,
and it exploded about 12 o'clock midnight. I then
returned to Indianapolis and reported to J. J. Mc-
Namara at his office, and he paid me $400 and ex-
penses, $200 and expenses for the Jersey City job
and $200 and expenses for the Pittsburg job.

"He then sent me to Omaha, Nebraska, and furnished me with a suit case. I was furnished with
the nitroglycerin by J. J. McNamara, together with
the two clock arrangements."

CHAPTER XXV

PAID $200 AND EXPENSES PER EXPLOSION

As McManigal continued with his confession we realized that it would be only a matter of patient work to verify everything he was telling us. Men would be sent to every hotel where he and Jim Mc-Namara had stopped, registers would be looked up and tracings made of the signatures of the two men. Hockin would be checked up in his movements also, and from the government weather bureau records would be found to verify the descriptions of weather conditions obtaining on the nights of the various explosions. If it snowed in this city the weather records would show whether McManigal was telling the truth. If it rained the records would say rain or show that McManigal had either made a mistake or was lying.

We lost no time in preparing for this work. It would require a big staff of careful, patient men. Registered letters and money orders could be traced through the post office department and the cashing of checks could be traced through the banks and their books. The cachés for dynamite and nitroglycerin would be uncovered and were subsequently uncovered. The purchase of materials for the infernal machines would be and were verified.

McManigal told where he bought twelve alarm clocks, a large purchase for a man not in the business, and we looked up this place and verified his statement. We take up his confession now at the point where he laid in a supply of the little clocks in Pittsburg.

The prisoner hidden away in Detective Reed's comfortable little home continued:

"At the time I was in Pittsburg, I purchased twelve of these clocks from a wholesale jewelry house on Eighth and Pennsylvania Avenue, I think. I purchased them from a lady clerk, paying, I think, $18 for them, which was 50 cents cheaper than what J. B. McNamara paid. I then proceeded to Omaha, Neb., and got the power house, down along the river. One charge was set off there. This was supposed to be the property of the Wisconsin Bridge Company, but it did not go by that name out there. I think it was called the Western Bridge Company. I was instructed by J. J. McNamara as to just where the job was, and where the stuff should be put. I immediately returned to Indianapolis, and received $200 and expenses from J. J. McNamara for this job. This was July 21st that the Omaha job came off.

"I came home, stopped off a day or two, and then went to Duluth, Minn., as per instructions given me when J. J. McNamara again furnished me with two cans of nitroglycerin, and two clocks. This stuff was in the cans when I got there. I went to Duluth and was told to get the coal hoist, a job being done by Heyl & Patterson. This was at Superior, across the river from Duluth. There were two charges here. The job was a success and I had no trouble in setting it off except that I had to watch the watchman. I was afraid of the dog.

"I returned to Indianapolis from Duluth, received my $200 and expenses, and was then directed by J. J. McNamara to proceed to Kansas City, Mo., and I would find some McClintic-Marshall work across the river. He then furnished me with a suitcase and three cans, making twelve quarts of nitroglycerin, and three clock arrangements. I proceeded there on August 23rd and stopped at a small lodging house, and then changed the next day, going to the Jefferson, registering there under the name of McGraw.

"While in Omaha, I registered at a hotel, the name of which I do not now remember, registering under the name of McGraw; also used the same name at Duluth, and also at Kansas City. I set one charge off in Kansas City. I carried this stuff down with me; there were high weeks around there. I made arrangements for three charges in the girders. The night I carried it down I expected to get in and make the three charges. After I had one can and two clocks carried in and placed in the high grass, I went back to the hotel, got the two cans and the other clock, and took them down there and carried them into the place with me. I saw something in the brush which I thought was a watchman and that he had seen me. I later learned it was a couple of negroes. I did not set it but left it there near the tree, but later on my way across the field discovered the watchman sitting right alongside the girders, and it would have been impossible for me to do anything. I then went back up to town, and the next day returned and tried to locate all this stuff where I had hidden it, but could not find the two clocks and one can of it, and I concluded that someone had picked it up, but I did locate two cans and one clock I had under the tree. That evening, I set these two cans and one clock between two big girders there, expecting them to go off about 9:30 or 10:00 o'clock p. m. that night when I was up in town. It failed to go off, however, for some cause or other. I heard no report. The next day I went down there and upon investigation saw that the stuff was still there. I went in there in broad daylight, took the clock arrangement from the cans and found that the batteries were not strong enough to make the spark. I detached the clock from it and went up to town, got a new battery at some electrical concern, and put a new battery in it, tested it, in the daytime, leaving the nitroglycerin between the girders. I rearranged it about 5 o'clock that evening. I saw nothing of the

watchman around. It went off that evening about
9:30 or 10:00 o'clock. This was August 23rd,
1910. I returned to Indianapolis, collected my $200
and expenses from J. J. McNamara, and we then
found we were out of nitroglycerin. J. J. McNamara told me I should look up somebody to buy
it from; that I should look up the fellow Hockin
had purchased it from. I went around to the towns
J. J. McNamara said I would find him at, one of
them New Albany, Ind. I went over to Albany
on the street car and returned to Indianapolis the
same day. I was instructed to look up a well-shooter
at Albany or Portland, Ind., named Kiser, but I
found that he had moved. A man at a livery barn
in Albany stated that he knew a man at Portland;
that I could probably find a well-shooter there. I
went to Portland and inquired. I saw a man on
the street who looked like a well-shooter and asked
him if he was a shooter. He directed me to a café
where I eventually met one. I made arrangements
to purchase nitroglycerin from him, discussed prices,
etc. He said he would sell it for $1.30 a quart. I
added another dollar to that myself, making it $2.30
a quart. I arranged with this man to buy 200 quarts
to be delivered whenever I called on him; he was
to meet me any place I designated.

"I then went to Muncie, Ind., and called at the
Muncie Transfer Company, and arranged to hire
a horse and wagon. In the meantime—I neglected
to state—J. J. McNamara had given me $500 to

buy the nitroglycerin.   After hiring the horse and
buggy from the Muncie Transfer Company, I proceeded to Albany, six miles away, and in the meantime telephoned this man and told him to meet
me in Albany with this amount of nitroglycerin,
which he did, delivering to me 200 quarts for which
I paid him.   After leaving him I drove back to
Muncie and buried the stuff alongside the road in
a cinder bed near Muncie on the road between Albany and Muncie, near the tracks of the Big Four.
I then returned the horse and wagon to the barn
and paid the man. I had a case that had been made
out of pasteboard to hold one big can containing
ten quarts.   I don't know who made this.   It was
given to me by J. J. McNamara at Indianapolis,
empty, and I was to transfer in this some of the
stuff. He also had a box arranged to carry with a
shawl strap and large enough to hold one of the
ten-quart cans.   These big cans hold ten quarts.
After returning the horse and wagon, I took two
cans with me back to Indianapolis, arriving there
in the afternoon.   I put it in the 5th floor of the
same building as McNamara's office.   McNamara's
office is located in the American Central Life Building on Monument Square, and on the 5th floor of
this building there is a vault that is controlled by
J. J. McNamara, and he furnished me with the
combination, which is as follows:

"20—40—60—35.

"I carried this stuff to the vault and placed it

in there. This was between August 24th and September 1st. My time for this transaction was $50, which was paid me by J. J. McNamara, together with my expenses."

CHAPTER XXVI

HOBOES BUILT FIRE OVER NITRO.

The reader may recall that it was this trip by McManigal to Portland, Ind., which gave us the first open path to the dynamiters. You may remember that my agency was called in immediately following the explosions in Peoria and East Peoria and that we found a can of nitroglycerin with clockwork attachment and an empty packing case with some loose sawdust. You may also remember how Operative H. A. Graves took a sample of the sawdust and how it proved the same sort of sawdust that was spilled in the road when Morehart transferred the nitroglycerin from his wagon to the rig hired by the purchaser who gave his name as "Mc-Graw."

When McManigal reached this part of his confession he was telling us things that we had already uncovered and we were certain that he was sticking to the truth and that he was telling the whole truth. The fact, even, that it had rained on the night of the Peoria explosions he did not neglect to tell us.

In that part of the confession to follow he did not tell us of an incident concerning the nitroglycerin

caché in the woods near Muncie. Our men sought
it out and found it. The leaves covering the explosive were charred as by a fire. A number of tramps
had picked out this spot to build a fire. The logs
were lit over the explosive. An inch or two more
of charring and it would have rained hobo fragments for a week in Indiana.

We now take McManigal to the Muncie caché.
His confession goes on in these words:

"I have neglected to state I had transferred all
of these 200 quarts of this stuff except four cans,
which would, of course, make 40 quarts. On my
way to the cinder pile, I overtook a man walking
along the railroad track and passed him. I looked
for the nitroglycerin in the cinders but was unable
to find all of it. I saw this party stop for a minute
or two and I quit searching. This man jumped
down on the road from the bridge and walked
underneath same and went away. It started to rain.
I had the two empty cases, already described, to
transport the two cans, and returned to Muncie,
Ind., to the Terminal Station, and telephoned J. J.
McNamara, knowing he would be in his office. The
next morning, I returned to the cinder pile, with a
shovel, but was unable to find anything there. I
thought perhaps some of the men employed at the
stone quarry directly across might have stolen it.
I returned to Indianapolis and discussed the matter
with J. J. McNamara.

"On my way from Kansas City, I stopped at Peoria, where I looked over work that J. J. Mc-Namara had instructed me to examine, same being material of the McClintic-Marshall Company. He directed me to see what shape they were in and what could be done to them. After getting this second lot of nitroglycerin, he told me to return to Peoria. (I had to make two trips to carry the thirty quarts.) There were three ten-quart cans. I took two quarts out of one ten-quart can and set it off in the yard of the Lucas Brothers foundry. After arranging the nitroglycerin in the McClintic-Marshall job, I returned to my hotel and was there when it exploded. I left the same night at midnight and went to Chicago. I stopped in Chicago a couple of days, and returned to Indianapolis, receiving $200 and my expenses.

"On October 9th, J. J. McNamara directed me to go to Worcester, Mass., and gave me two four-quart cans, which he had all prepared and directed me to set it under the Phœnix Bridge Company job at that point. I did this job and then went to Boston, and got the train to Springfield, Mass., as I was instructed to look over the Court House and Tower there, which I did.

"I then went to Philadelphia, having instructions to look over some work the McClintic-Marshall people were doing there, some elevated railroad work for the Philadelphia and Reading railroad. I looked it over and I concluded it would be a very

serious matter to blow this up as there were too
many tenement houses in the vicinity, which unquestionably would be affected by the explosion.

"Returning to Indianapolis, I received my $200
and expenses from J. J. McNamara for the
Worcester job. He asked me about the Springfield job. I said I was afraid of it as it was next
door to a police station. He said, 'We'll have to
get that—that's all there is to it.' "

CHAPTER XXVII

THE LOS ANGELES MASSACRE ORDERED

The dynamiters had met with such success that they were now ready to attempt the elimination of General Harrison Gray Otis, his home, his family, his business and his employees in Los Angeles. If this intended massacre did not bring victory for the conspirators the conspirators were ready to follow it with the complete destruction of the city of Los Angeles and the destruction of the Panama Canal with it. They had enough dynamite and nitroglycerin to blow up half the cities of the country and enough men to lay the mines.

McManigal now tells of the preliminaries for the Los Angeles job as follows:

"Along in June, J. B. McNamara and I went to Indianapolis together. Had a conversation with J. J. McNamara and J. B. McNamara; I can't fix the exact date, but I think it was immediately after my return from Pittsburg, July 14th or 21st. J. B. McNamara said he was going to the Coast; and he was going to get in touch with a fellow called 'The Old Man' (who I afterwards found out was

a man called Tveitmoe), and Clancy. He told me
that he had been instructed by J. J. McNamara.
When he was ready to go to the Coast, he and I
went to Chicago on the same train. He was then
on his way. I asked him what was coming off out
there. He said that the whole damn thing was no
good out there; that they were going to make a
big clean-up; that there was plenty of money put
up. He said it was planned that he go to the Coast
and I stay here. This was decided in a conference
J. J. McNamara and J. B. McNamara and I had
at the office in Indianapolis.

"J. B. McNamara put up a proposition to the
parties in California that they buy the stuff here
instead of out there. When he was leaving he had
two suitcases. He had clocks in one, I think a
dozen, and clothes in the other. He told me that
he used the stuff they bought out there on the
Times. This statement came out in a discussion
as to what quantity he used. He said he used eight
sticks on the Times. The clocks referred to may
have been clocks I purchased in Pittsburg. (Mc-
Manigal could not remember all the conversation
between J. B. McNamara and J. J. McNamara at
Indianapolis, just previous to the departure of the
former for California.)

"While J. B. McNamara was in California, I
saw an account of something that happened at
Spokane; then there was one around Oakland. I
asked J. J. McNamara if he had received any word

from the 'fellow on the Coast,' meaning, of course, his brother, and he knew who I meant. He said, 'No, I have not.' I said I saw a couple of accounts. He said, 'Yes, I did too, but I don't know whether it was him or who it was.' It ran along a while and I asked him again if he had heard anything. He said he had a letter. In the meantime I had gotten in touch with Hockin, and he asked me where J. B. McNamara was. I told him I did not know. The next time J. J. McNamara and I talked about J. B. was when I later asked him if he had received any word. He said, yes, he received a letter from 'Frisco, in which J. B. McNamara said, 'It now reads "Times for News." It will read "News for the Times."' This was about two or three weeks before the explosion.

"The next time I talked with J. J. McNamara about J. B. McNamara on the Coast was when I saw an account of the Times explosion. I was in Chicago at the time. I bought a paper and read same. The next time I went to Indianapolis, he said, '—————— ————! See what those fellows are doing out there!' I said, 'I wonder if that is that fellow.' He said, 'I don't know; I guess it must be. It was the Times they wanted and got.' I expressed the opinion that it was too bad so many people being killed. He said, 'By God! That ought to make them come across.' I said, 'I suppose he is on his way back. If that's the case he must be well on his way with such a thing like that happening.' He said, 'I suppose so. If he isn't he is well under cover.'

"J. J. McNamara instructed me not to come to their office too damn often. He said, 'I don't know who the hell is around here.' He was quite nervous at that time. He said he thought then there would be somebody looking around and he suspected a fellow over in another office building. I saw there had been changes made in the office—a general cleaning up of cuts, etc. I then returned to Chicago and kept under cover.

"I first heard of J. B. returning about the third or fourth of November, when there was a telephone call at my house, but I was not at home. My wife answered the phone and the party said, 'Is Mac home?' 'No.' The party then said, 'Tell Mac his friend Mr. Clark wants to see him at 11 o'clock at the Briggs Hotel.' I went down there and looked over the register and there was no such name on same. (I knew who it was I was to meet as I heard him use that name before.) He was talking to a stranger to me. After the latter left him, we walked down the street somewhere. The moment I met him he told me that he had seen him (meaning J. B.) and he (J. J. McNamara) said, '————————! Things are red hot. There's a hell of a smear around there.' I said, 'Is he clear? Is he out of the way?' He said, 'He is away, but he is not clear yet.' I tried to get out of him where he was, but he would not tell me. He wanted to know if I had anything around the house. I told him no, I did not. He said if I had I should get rid of it. We entered an office building down the street. I stood inside the lobby while he went upstairs. This office building, I think, is on Dearborn Street, near Van Buren. He remained upstairs a few minutes, then we went toward Madison Street, had lunch and J. J. McNamara told me he knew where the fellow was that he had seen (meaning J. B.). I asked him how he looked and he said, 'Pretty good.'

"He asked me if I was going hunting, and I said, 'Yes.' I had talked hunting with him for some time previous. 'Everything is all arranged to go hunting. There are five of us going and there is room for another fellow if one wants to go.' He said the fellow had no gun, and I said the fellow could use my gun. I also told him I thought it would be the best thing for him; a trip in the woods would be a good thing for him. He said he would put the proposition up to him and let me know. I left J. J. McNamara at Van Buren and Dearborn Streets, with the understanding that I was to hear from him. I then went home. That evening, I understood he was to go somewhere on 55th Street, saying he wanted to see a party there.

"That evening Hockin telephoned me at my home and wanted to know when I had seen the 'big fellow.' I told him I had seen him about noon and he said he was going to 55th Street. He said, 'I

had an appointment with him and have been waiting for him and was wondering what became of
him.' He wanted to know what I was doing. I
was going hunting, I told him. That was about the
2nd or 3rd of November. He asked me who was
going along. I said, some fellows from Kenosha
and a fellow from Chicago. He wanted to know
if I had seen anything of the 'queer guy,' meaning
J. B. McNamara. I said, 'No, I have not seen him,
but I have heard.' He said he wished he could see
me or have a talk with me; that he could give me
some good pointers or something to that effect. He
wanted to know when I was leaving home. I said,
Saturday, when I went to Kenosha for my license,
and was going to leave Monday for the woods.
In a way that I knew this fellow was coming, J. J.
McNamara sent me a telegram worded in such a
way I knew what was meant. This telegram was
from Indianapolis. I endeavored to arrange for a
gun for him, but could not obtain it. I then went
to Kenosha and met the parties I was to meet there,
and made application for license. J. B. McNamara
met us on Sunday morning, having come up on Saturday night, calling me over the 'phone, as he had
the number of the house I was stopping at. I met
him at the hotel. J. J. McNamara had told me
that J. B.'s name would be Frank Sullivan and I
must get into the habit of calling him 'Sully'; he
told me this in Chicago. We entered the bar at a
hotel in Kenosha and had a few drinks."

CHAPTER XXVIII

JIM MCMAMARA'S STORY OF THE CRIME

Just how much humanity there was in the breast of either of the McNamara brothers is pretty well shown in their cold-blooded handling of affairs immediately following the wholesale murder in Los Angeles. There was never a suggestion of remorse on the part of either, no ghost of any one of the twenty-one murdered men and boys ever haunted either of them.

Jim McNamara told McManigal of his Los Angeles job with the same casual account of detail he might have used in relating the story of one of his many sprees.

McManigal's confession thus describes Jim McNamara's tale of his dreadful deed:

"I first had a talk with J. B. McNamara when we arrived. He said, 'When we get into the woods, I can tell you all.'

"When we did get to the woods, he told me that when he got out there he got in touch with Clancy at San Francisco. J. B. seemed to be very sore about the layout on the Coast. He did not like the fellows he was working with. He said he was working with a fellow named Schmitty and a fellow named Caplan. He said Clancy introduced him to Tveitmoe; that the latter introduced him to Schmitty and Caplan, and that Schmitty and Caplan had been doing the work around that part of the country, that Tveitmoe wanted him to take the light end of it, and instead of that Schmitty gave him orders.

"J. B. McNamara told me what a time they had getting the stuff, at the Giant Powder Mills. He wanted to drop the proceedings. Schmitty, it seems, was the main man. He said they rented a launch, but none of them knew how to run it, although Schmitty and Caplan thought they did. In loading the launch, they put all the boxes in burlap in the front end of the launch, and the rudder on the other end was clear out of water. Schmitty was engineer and instead of making headway, they made 'backway.'

"Schmitty started the launch into the shore near the Giant Powder Company, and while Schmitty and Caplan got out of the boat into the skiff, a wave came up and started the boat out.

"They got a room after landing on the Frisco side and rented a house in which they stored the stuff. When they got the stuff they had to make a deposit, and they covered the name on the boat with red tape. The stuff was signed for in J. B. Bryce's name. They placed part of the stuff in

the house they rented and took a part of it to Oakland. There were taxicabs, high living, wine, etc.
He said that he was down there and looked over
the situation at Los Angeles. He returned again to
see Schmitty and Schmitty gave him the address of
some woman down there who runs a rooming house.
Anyway, Schmitty wanted to go to Los Angeles
also. He did not want Schmitty to go down, so he
called on 'The Old Man' (meaning Tveitmoe) and
said, 'I want you to call that fellow off (meaning
Schmitty). I don't think he ought to go down
there, and if he goes down there I am not going
down.' 'The Old Man' told him to go on about his
business and he would see that Schmitty and Caplan
stayed there, because just as soon as anything happened, Schmitty would run right up to Tveitmoe's
office and out would come the cash. Schmitty told
J. B. McNamara, 'You are to get $200 with your
expenses; that is the arrangement made.' I don't
recall whether he said he himself made the arrangements with Caplan and Caplan with Schmitty, but
the names of Caplan and Schmitty were mentioned.
The men were always paid by Tveitmoe. He said
he stopped at the Roslin Hotel in Los Angeles. He
tried to get in the building two or three times but
was unsuccessful; that is, the Times Building. He
told me that he had three places picked: 'Otis's
house, Zeehandelaar's house, and the Times. He
said that he had a hell of a time passing the
watchman in front of the Times. He said the

watchman was stationed at the entrance or back end of the alley. Some kid came to the door as he came in and he asked him about the publication room or something. He made a plant, and got out of there right away, going back to Frisco, laying over for four days in Frisco, stopping at the Argonaut Hotel. He told me about the time he was having with the fast women and others in San Francisco all the time, and also about the woman who kept the rooming house where he hung out. This was prior to the Los Angeles explosion. He came back and stopped at the Argonaut Hotel when he came back from Los Angeles. He told me about the money Tveitmoe still owes him, there never having been a settlement. When he returned to Frisco he got in touch with Schmitty and Caplan, and he had to wait four days to get his money, and then Schmitty gave it to him; or either Schmitty or Tveitmoe gave it to him, amounts unknown. He immediately started back. I don't know where he stopped on his way. There was some fellow who came part way here, but J. B. McNamara did not mention his name.

"I then returned to Chicago and wrote J. J. McNamara a letter.

"A couple of days later I received a telegram from J. B. McNamara, signing 'Frank,' stating, 'Leave on 2:45 Monon train.' I went to Indianapolis, and J. J. stated that I would have to go to Los Angeles. I said, 'That's a hell of a trip.' He

said, 'It will be three days and three nights' ride.'
He wanted me to go out there and see if we could
get any more of the Times Building (the auxiliary
plant), and also the Llewellyn plant (Llewellyn
Iron Works) and the Baker Iron Works. J. B.
McNamara said, 'I wish I were going along with
you. I would go back there in a minute. But this
fellow don't seem to think that I ought to go back
there.' This was said in J. J. McNamara's office
and in J. J. McNamara's presence. I said, 'If you
want to go, go ahead.' I told him I would not go
unless I had my transportation and expense and
everything on the train. He said, 'That will be all
right; that will be attended to.' I went out alone.
On arrival there, I did not connect with any one.
J. J. McNamara had given me the information as
to where everything was and what was wanted. I
carried 12 quarts with me. One was a ten-quart
can in the pasteboard arrangement and two quarts
in my valise. I gave it to the porter on the train
and he put it in a closet in the end of the car.

"I left about the 11th or 12th via the Overland
Limited, at 10:16 in the evening. No one was with
me when I left. I got the dope from J. J. Mc-
Namara as had been previously arranged. I had
two or three clocks, all arranged for use, with me.
I went to a hotel, and then looked over the Llewellyn Iron Works, and visited the auxiliary plant
of the Times. J. B. McNamara was able to tell
me definitely where these places were located and

conditions about the same. I found the Times place was well watched. I then visited the Llewellyn plant and tried to get into the yards, and set the 12 quarts along the outside of the building, being unable to get inside. I then went to my hotel and checked out. I looked the Baker Brothers place over, but decided not to bother it. I stopped at the Rosslyn Hotel under the name of J. M. McKee, LaCrosse, Wis.

"When I left Los Angeles, I went to San Francisco, and got in touch with Clancy at the Labor Temple. I stopped at the Argonaut Hotel.

"J. B. McNamara said to me that by going out there and setting off this stuff, if the detectives were still on their trail, they would think the dynamiters were still out there.

"In conversation with Clancy, whom I had never seen before, but whom I talked to when I was in Frisco, I said, 'When you see The Old Man, you can tell him that "Christmas present" was delivered' (meaning by 'The Old Man,' Tveitmoe).

"On arrival in Chicago, I remained here until after New Year's. Then I saw J. J. McNamara at Indianapolis. J. B. McNamara was present at our interview. He expressed his disappointment at my failure to carry out his instructions, saying, 'You should have gotten a bunch of that soup in the Times and given them a shaking up.' I said, 'My God! It did not look good to me. It looked like suicide.' They said if I had carried out the thing the way they told me to it would have averted suspicion from them and myself. He paid me my time and expenses, amounting to $400.

"J. J. McNamara stated, 'We will keep on one job and work on that one (meaning by that, not jumping from coast to coast and job to job), but take one town and see what we can do with that, and if anything can be done it will be done, and if nothing can be done, we will take another job.' J. B. McNamara was present at this meeting. This remark was made in the evening at J. J.'s office. The only time he would see us at his office was at night.

"J. J. McNamara said to me, 'I want you to go up there and clean up that Milwaukee job. It is a coal hoist at the Milwaukee Fuel Company, the Heyl-Patterson Company erecting it.' McNamara had everything arranged, gave me a suitcase, and I went to Milwaukee, stopping at the Acme Hotel, under the name of Foster or Fisher (I forget which). I had no trouble in setting it off. It went off all right and I had no trouble in getting away. I reported to J. J. McNamara and received $200 and expenses. He then said, 'I want you to go to Omaha and get that Court House there.' In the meantime J. B. McNamara had gone to Columbus, Ind. I did not go with him. It had been arranged that when things were ready with me at Omaha I should telegraph J. J. McNamara, 'Please forward one hundred to Lincoln, Nebraska.' That meant the other fellow was to go ahead and set his off the same night. I sent it from the Northwestern Railroad depot in Omaha; then set it off. I was stopping at the Murray House under the name of G. Fisher.

"Returning from Omaha, I reported to J. J. McNamara, got my money, seeing him at night, and he told me I should go to Boston and then come back through Springfield, Mass., and see what I could do on the tower there. He said he wanted me to do this right away. I asked him where J. B. McNamara was. He said he was in Chicago the other day. He had telephoned my wife. At Indianapolis that night I got in touch with Hockin. He had seen an account of the Columbus and Omaha affairs. I asked him how things looked. He said everything looked all right.

"Arrangements were made for me to go to Boston, and J. J. McNamara had the stuff ready for me. I took 40 pounds of dynamite. I don't know where it came from. I carried it all in one suitcase. We discussed the matter. I had no trouble in setting the stuff off there. I stopped under the name of G. Fisher or G. Foster (I have forgotten which) at the Hinkley Hotel.

"I returned from Springfield to Detroit where McNamara wanted me to look at several places for him:

"Detroit Breech & Steel Company.

"South Dearborn & Michigan Central Railway

of Detroit (South Dearborn is a suburb of Detroit on the M. C. R. R.).

"Whitehead & Kahel.

"Breecher & Michigan Central Shops.

"American Bridge Company.

"Russel Wheel & Foundry Company, Campau Avenue, Detroit.

"I reported the above O. K. to J. J. McNamara —that these could be gotten if wanted. He located J. B. McNamara, and said to me, 'You had better get ready and go right back there now.' I said, 'I don't want to go back there. I am going to run into Chicago.' I said to J. B., 'What have you got on?' 'I haven't got anything on,' he said. J. J. McNamara said, 'Are you going down to see that fellow?' 'Yes, I thought I would.' (I don't know who he meant.) He said, 'You go down and see about that and make up some of those clocks.'

"I was to meet J. B. McNamara at Toledo Tuesday evening, which I did. We met at Toledo, and intended going over to Detroit.

"Relative to the explosion at West Baden, J. B. McNamara told me he did the job and it was unionized the next morning before the explosion was reported at Indianapolis.

"I neglected to state about the explosion at South Chicago. I was called to Indianapolis by J. J. McNamara and he said that Chicago had a job up there, and that Hockin was going up to investigate it and would be back in a day or two. Hockin had been up there and got in touch with somebody and inspected the job. J. B. McNamara came to my house and told me where to go, he following instructions issued by J. J. McNamara. We went out one Sunday evening, looked it over and decided to blow up. We took the 2:45 train for Indianapolis and got the stuff and returned Monday night with it. We got back about 8 o'clock that evening, stopping at the 'Best' Hotel, No. 78-80 Van Buren Street. We left the stuff in the basement at my house. The next day I came over to my place in the forenoon, and made up the clock in my house. We used dynamite for this job. J. J. McNamara wanted the smokestack hit. We found the place better guarded, however, than on our first visit and after debating it between ourselves, returned the next evening and found conditions the same. On Friday night we took the stuff out and after consideration put it on the outside of the fence, where it went off.

"There is some soup planted on the far west side of Indianapolis in a barn owned by a fellow named Jones, from whom McNamara rented it. Go west on Washington Street to end of street car line, go on walking same direction, pass concrete bridge, follow road, continue until you reach Big Four tracks. Just beyond tracks on the right hand side is a barn. The dynamite is in the barn in a piano box. This was placed here by J. B. McNamara and myself in January, 1911. This was pro-

cured down in Ohio in Bloomville. The fellow
from whom I secured the dynamite is described:

"Forty-five to 48 years, full sandy beard, 5 feet
10 inches, shabbily dressed.

"M. J. Young, No. 386 Harrison Avenue, Boston, is business agent of local No. 7, Structural Iron
Workers. He is the man who arranged to have the
Springfield stuff set off. I told him that J. J. Mc-
Namara had sent me down there to meet him and
he was to tell me what he wanted done. I met
him at headquarters, No. 368 Harrison Avenue.
He wanted a fellow slugged. I told him I did not
do that kind of business.

"Dynamite planted on the 5th floor of building
where J. J. McNamara has an office in the vault,
combination of which is: 20—40—80—35. There
might be some in the basement of the building.
There is some stuff stored in Tiffin, Ohio, in a
shanty off of Perry Street, back of wagon works on
my father's place, at a stone quarry. It is stored in
a shanty. There is considerable of it there."

CHAPTER XXIX

BURNS LANDS THE MAN HIGHER UP

We kept J. B. McNamara and Ortie McManigal under close guard. We knew that J. J. McNamara would be anxious to hear from his brother and McManigal, that an article had appeared in the Associated Press stating that James Sullivan and Ortie McManigal had been arrested as safe blowers at Detroit and taken to Chicago, and that this would probably be seen by him. I called up McManigal's wife, and introduced the following piece of subterfuge:

Calling up Harrison ———, a woman's voice replied. I said, "Is this Harrison ———?" "Yes," was the answer. "Well," I said, "you don't know me, but I have just received a letter from a friend of mine at Detroit, and I will read it to you."

She said, "Who are you?" I said, "You don't know me, nor do I care to give my name, but I will read you this letter, and perhaps that will enlighten you. I'm sure it's Greek to me, and I don't know anything about it." She said, "Very well." Then I began: "Dear Jack: Immediately on receipt of this letter, call up Harrison ——— and tell the woman there"—and I said, "are you the woman?"

—she said, "Yes, yes, I'm the woman." "Tell the woman there that her husband and his friends were arrested in Detroit for safe blowing, and as nothing could be proved against them they were discharged, and they are now in Windsor, Canada."

"Good! Good!" shouted Mrs. McManigal over the 'phone. "My God, but I'm glad to hear that. That's splendid news. Oh, I'm so glad they have gotten away."

"Now," I said, "listen to the rest of it. Tell her to go to a friend of theirs. Now it doesn't say who the friend is."

"Oh, that's all right; I know who it is. Go ahead; go ahead," she said. I continued, "Go to a friend of theirs and tell him to give her $500, and for her then to return home and await a further message from her husband." I said, "Do you understand that?"

"Yes, perfectly; I understand what they mean, and I will leave to-night."

I said, "Is there any word that you want to send back to them?"

"Yes, tell them I will leave to-night and that I will get back about to-morrow night."

I said, "All right. Good-bye."

"Good-bye."

We put a shadow on Mrs. McManigal, and she immediately left, as she stated she would, for Indianapolis. When she reached there she saw J. J. McNamara and told him the story, as we subsequently learned. While it relieved him to some extent, he was not altogether reassured. Why he was not developed later on, and was an important feature that McManigal had entirely overlooked in the first part of his confession. J. J. McNamara had an understanding with his brother and McManigal that if at any time they got into trouble they were to write or wire a certain post office box, No. 1, in Indianapolis, which had been obtained under another name. Therefore, McNamara thought, if all this were true that Mrs. McManigal had stated, why did not the two men comply with his direction to notify him through the post office box. Our "shadows" at Indianapolis constantly reported that J. J. McNamara was extremely nervous, constantly testing himself, and looking about in an effort to uncover them.

After the Los Angeles explosion, J. J. McNamara showed a picture of me, cut from a magazine, to Ortie McManigal and J. B. McNamara, and said to them: "Look out for this fellow. If ever anybody gets you at all, it will be this guy."

Finally, the officers, accompanied by Assistant District Attorney Robert Ford, arrived in Chicago, and we promptly arranged for requisition papers for James B. McNamara and Ortie McManigal from the State of Illinois. I then arranged that when the signal was given they should leave Reed's house in an automobile and drive to Joliet, Ill., and there board the fast train for Los Angeles.

We proceeded to Indianapolis, and Assistant District Attorney Robert Ford, Detective Sergeant Hoosick, and myself promptly got in touch with the Superintendent of Police at the Indianapolis Police Department, and the Chief of Detectives.

Both of them we knew as honest, conscientious, capable officials, and had no hesitation in promptly laying the whole matter before them. The Superintendent said that he would aid in every possible way he could, after being assured that we had the evidence. Assistant District Attorney Ford then called on Governor Marshall—now Vice-President Marshall. He inquired into the situation, and assuring himself as to the legal questions involved, promptly performed his duty and issued a warrant for J. J. McNamara, which was promptly placed in the hands of the Superintendent of Police Martin and Chief of Detectives.

He then detailed two detectives to go to the office of the Iron Workers, and requested me to go along and designate the man. I did so, and when we reached the offices of the Structural Iron Workers, we found them in counsel. It was apparent to any person that something ominous had happened that caused a depression of the spirits of every man about that table. When one of us rapped on the door it was opened by J. J. McNamara. The officer said: "I am a Detective Sergeant from Headquarters, and I want to see J. J. McNamara and Herbert S. Hockin."

McNamara said, "I'm the man."

"Well," said the Sergeant, "the Chief would like to see you."

McNamara said, "Very well." He walked over and had a talk with President Ryan, of the Iron Workers, and said to him: "They're after me. What had I better do about it?" Ryan advised him to go ahead. McNamara put on his coat and hat. He then made an excuse that he wanted to leave the keys to his desk there, and this was the only slip that occurred in the entire arrangement, for in that time J. J. McNamara was permitted to divest himself of the keys of the lower vault found in the cellar.

We then walked to Police Headquarters, where the officer delivered Hockin and J. J. McNamara to the Superintendent and Chief of Detectives Holtz. Holtz read the requisition papers and the warrant to J. J. McNamara, and then conducted him before the Desk Sergeant, where they booked him just as they would any other prisoner and then locked him up. Later we took him before Judge Collins, the Judge before whom all requisitions were taken. The Judge examined the papers carefully, and finding they were regular and all right so stated, and then said that the next requisite was the identification of J. J. McNamara as the man named in the warrant. McNamara promptly spoke up: "I admit that I'm the man named in that warrant."

"Very well, then," said the Judge, "the only thing

left for me to do is to turn you over to the State of California."

Detective Sergeant Hoosick then conducted J. J. McNamara to an automobile that was in waiting, as it was feared that the hidden dynamite at Indianapolis might possibly be resorted to if there was any delay in removing McNamara.

He was accompanied on his trip by Detective Sergeant Hoosick of Los Angeles, Detective Sergeants Guy Biddinger and William Reed, and Charles J. Smith of our Chicago office.

I would like to say here, in passing, that when I finally made up my mind to round up the McNamaras and McManigal, I called on Captain Steve Woods, who was then in charge of Detective Headquarters at Chicago, and who, by the way, was one of the best and most efficient men they ever had in that position. I explained to him that I was about to round up the dynamiters of the Los Angeles Times and that I wanted to have detailed to me Detective Sergeants Guy Biddinger and William Reed. He promptly stated that he would detail them, and would notify them to respond when called upon, and that he would aid in any way he possibly could in their apprehension. I then instructed my son, Raymond, that when the arrest took place the men should not be taken to the station-house, but should be taken to a private house—Reed's.

After J. J. McNamara left in the automobile, I then, in company with Mayor Schrank, Superintendent of Police Highland, Chief of Detectives Holtz, and Harry M. Friend, of the Chicago American, led them to the Jones barn, which was in the outskirts of Indianapolis. On reaching there we found Jones, who conducted us to the barn. On opening the door we found the piano box described by Ortie McManigal, and with the keys taken from the pocket of J. B. McNamara, I unlocked the box in their presence. In the piano box was found a second box, and on opening that it was found half-filled with sawdust and a large quantity of sticks of dynamite and a can of nitroglycerin. The original brand on the wrappers of the dynamite had been destroyed.

Before this, we went to the offices of the Structural Iron Workers and made a search of them. We opened the office vault, but found nothing incriminating.

While searching there, the janitor of the building came to me and said, "Mr. Burns, do you want to search the vault in the cellar?" I replied that we did, and he promptly conducted us to a specially constructed vault in the cellar of the building, but for this he did not have the keys. Superintendent Highland was about to wrench the lock, when a person calling himself a lawyer showed up on the scene, and remonstrated and denied the right of the Superintendent to open that vault under the search warrant the Superintendent then had. Mr. Highland, wanting to be perfectly fair, left an

officer in charge of the vault, returned to the Police
Station and secured a special search warrant for
that vault.   When he returned, the lock was
wrenched from the door, and on entering, accompanied by the janitor, we found two large packages
of dynamite, weighing 92 pounds, with the corners
conveniently torn for the purpose of inserting the
wire from clock bombs.   They were wrapped exactly like those described by our operatives at Chicago as having been carried by J. B. McNamara
and Ortie McManigal.

In addition, we found 14 alarm clocks exactly
like those used on the bombs at Peoria and Los
Angeles, together with a large amount of fulminating caps and all the paraphernalia that went to
make up the bombs, as well as a large quantity of
fuse.   We also found a great mass of correspondence which, on investigation, was found to be letters
from various business agents throughout the country to J. J. McNamara requesting that the wrecking
crew be sent them to carry on certain work, indicat-
ing, of course, dynamiting jobs.

McNamara, in his methodical way, and for some
unknown reason, replied to these letters, stating
they would arrive there at a certain time, and then
transcribed the answers on the back of the letters
and filed them away.   Many persons, since the trial
at Indianapolis, have expressed the greatest surprise
that a man engaged in such nefarious work should
have been guilty of such an asinine trick.   The reply

to this is, that McNamara had no idea that the persons engaged in running down the dynamiters of the Los Angeles Times would *dare* to intrude into the sanctum of the Structural Iron Workers' Union.

A tremendous effort was then made by the union's lawyer to prevent the correspondence from being carried away. He had evidently received a "hunch" from some person other than J. J. McNamara as to how important it was, but thanks to Superintendent Highland and his assistants, nothing was overlooked and it was all carried to the Police Station. The following day we carried the dynamite and the nitroglycerin into the country, on a second visit, and buried the nitroglycerin and cachéd the dynamite, care being taken to mark everything for identification.

Superintendent Highland demanded admission to the safe in the office of the Structural Iron Workers, which was denied him, and he then sent for an expert safeman, who drilled the safe and opened it.

In the meantime, the partisans of J. J. McNamara held a counsel and decided that they ought to get busy and put up a defense. They expressed, in the loudest way they could, and with as much noise as possible, the conviction that J. J. McNamara had been kidnapped and the offices of the Union had been unlawfully invaded. President Ryan also made the charge that a sum of money that was in a drawer in the office had disappeared, and intimated that some of the officers must have taken it.

I then proceeded to Tiffin, Ohio, called on the Chief of Police, and together we went to the barn of Ortie McManigal's father, in the outskirts of Tiffin, and here we found a box of dynamite.

I then proceeded to Toledo, Ohio, and at the railroad station, in company with Chief of Police Harry Knapp, found J. B. McNamara's suitcase, which had been used for carrying explosives, and which was thoroughly soaked with nitroglycerin.

We returned to Indianapolis and sent for Morehart, who hurried from Muncie, and identified the nitroglycerin that had been found in the Jones barn as part of that sold by him to Ortie McManigal. He also identified the can. Our operatives and the Police at Indianapolis made a search of the room of J. J. McNamara, and there found one of the time clocks such as they used on the bomb, and several other incriminating articles.

The newspaper men, immediately after the arrest at Indianapolis, strongly urged me to give them some details of the incriminating evidence found, which I declined to do, on the ground that it was not fair to the prosecuting attorney nor fair to the defendant that we discuss that previous to his trial, but within a short time they came to me with a statement made by Samuel Gompers, President of the American Federation of Labor, who was interviewed at Pittsburgh, and who intimated that it was a "frame-up," by myself, and that the dynamite had been planted where it was found.

Offended by the slander that had been uttered by Gompers, and knowing that it was calculated to inflame the minds of some irresponsible persons who might seek to revenge themselves on me personally, I went into details and pointed out that if it was a frame-up, J. J. McNamara, his brother, J. B. McNamara, and Ortie McManigal had framed it up, as the keys which opened the box at the Jones barn—Jones being a member of the Structural Iron Workers' Union—were taken from the pocket of J. B. McNamara. We found where the keys had been purchased at Indianapolis. The keys which unlocked the box in the McManigal barn at Tiffin had also been taken from the pocket of J. B. McNamara. Therefore, all the plans had been shown, conclusively, to have been arranged by J. J. McNamara, J. B. McNamara and Ortie Mc-Manigal.

Gompers subsequently came to Indianapolis, and again denounced me in the strongest terms, and subsequently many of the labor organizations throughout the country passed resolutions condemning me, and the same was taken up by Socialists throughout the country, who, on the street corners, uttered the same denunciations and the same charges. The following Labor Day, throughout the country, was dedicated to the McNamara Brothers, and collections taken up all over the country. In the parades American flags were carried through the streets, and the coins and contributions solicited were tossed into the American flags. I was the recipient of hundreds of anonymous letters denouncing me and threatening my life.

CHAPTER XXX

PETER CURRAN'S CLASSIC LETTER

The detective story of fiction would end with the arrests of the guilty men in the case, but in real life the detective who keeps a clear head on his shoulders knows that before him is one of the hardest stretches of his task. He is morally certain of the guilt of the men he has placed in jail, but he must have enough evidence to make twelve jurors be certain of their guilt also or his work will go for nothing. Moreover, he will have to watch with the eye of a hawk to see that his witnesses are not bribed or spirited away from him. He must see to it that his assistants are not tempted with large sums of money to "throw" the case and in the dynamiting trials we had the further job of preventing the bribery of jurors.

We did not slow up for a moment in this work, for in this masked war against society there were, besides the McNamaras, the 38 union "leaders" afterward found guilty of conspiracy in the Federal trials at Indianapolis. It was no one-man conspiracy but was nation-wide.

While the McNamaras and McManigal were being hurried to Los Angeles I sent a careful operative post haste to Cincinnati and to the little home of the McNamaras in Quarry Street in the Cumminsville section. A search warrant was secured and in the McNamara home he found more electrical apparatus and letters referring to various dynamiting jobs done at the order of J. J.

I and my operatives uncovered the various depots for explosives established by the dynamiters besides the one I told of in the Jones barn. We traced the piano box found in this caché back to its maker and connected its purchase with the union officials.

In Muncie, Ind., we found a house rented by the dynamiters for the storage of nitroglycerin and here was required patient work by my operatives. The last of the explosive had been used from this depot, but the floor of the room, where the cans of nitro had been placed, showed the greasy stains from the sweating of the tins. That floor would make an exhibit in court. The owner of the house was about to rent it and the tenant was anxious to get into the place. That meant scrubbing the greasy floor, of course. Scrubbing the floor would have meant the wiping out of the evidence. There was one way to preserve it. We were rather shy of money, having spent a great deal in the investigation, and I could not afford to buy the house. We made a dicker with the owner and agreed to give him a new floor for the room if he gave us the old. This agreed to, my operatives numbered each board of the floor, after making photographs of it, and took it up and carried it to a place of safety.

Occasionally an operative at work on the case would develop material that would raise a smile. We did not have any time to spare for a good laugh, however absurd a thing might be, but funny things occasionally do happen even in the business of detecting crime and criminals. Investigator No. 31 was sent to an open lot at the corner of Morgan and Van Buren Streets, Chicago, to dig for a box McManigal had buried as a handy caché for explosives. Digging for dynamite is a ticklish business. The tip of a pick or the edge of a shovel might strike hard enough to rip a hole in the ground and send the investigator into the air. No. 31 gingerly went at his task and finally found a box at about the depth described by McManigal. Elated, he rushed to the nearest telephone and informed our Chicago office of the find. My son, Raymond, the manager of the office, hurried to the scene to witness the uncovering of the box of dynamite. The broken earth was removed and the box drawn from the hole. The lid was lifted and instead of dynamite was found the body of a dog. Some youngster, perhaps, had given his dead pet a decent burial.

The dog was reinterred, No. 31 looked sheepish, Raymond returned to his office and a day's work went for a laugh.

From a collection of many letters in the correspondence of the dynamiters and their friends there was none that equalled the friendly epistle written by one Peter Curran to Jim McNamara. This letter was found in the McNamara home. The envelope showed that it had been mailed in Chicago, June 7, 8 a. m., 1909.

Here is the classic:

"Chicago, Ill. June 6, 1909.
"Dear friend Mc:

"I received your postal and was glad to hear from you. I am still at the Rosena Hotel. The night cleark that was thur wen you were ther got into a sirkes girl's room and Miss Horton found it out and fired him. Jim and Eral is working at bumpers. They can get pleanty orders if they can do them cheap anough. Everything is about the same around hear. Old Casper is moping around with the rat trap as usual. Mrs. Anderson have a very sore foot with roontisen. Mrs. Wright moved. I sean Willie and he gave me his address and said to send it to you wen I rote. 6817 So. Chicago Ave. It was very cold hear all spring. Have not much new to tell you lot of building gowing up. You must excuse me for not writing sooner. Let me now how you are getting along and how is your mother is and if you are tire of Cincinatia yet?   "Your truly

"Peter Curran
"Rosena Hotel
"corner 18th St. and Wabaush."

While my operatives were in the Cumminsville section of Cincinnati, securing correspondence and information for the preparation of the case for the people, they hunted up the records, church and civil, of the McNamara family. My purpose was to leave nothing of their lives covered. For the mother of these two prisoners we had nothing but sympathy. She had ever been a hard working, religious, good woman and in her old age she was to suffer the sorrow of having two of her sons bring her head down in disgrace.

But the mother of the McNamaras had had sorrow and bitter sorrow before. Her husband was a drunken and quarrelsome man and sank into viciousness. He was arrested charged with a crime of such a nature that it can only be referred to as moral turpitude. He was convicted and sentenced to prison for life. Through the efforts of J. J. McNamara he was released from prison about 1909. He never returned to his home and is said to be living in Columbus, Ohio. Before J. J. McNamara and J. B. McNamara were arrested they are said to have supplied him with funds sufficient to keep him going.

In the records of St. Patrick's Church, Cumminsville, we found that John Joseph McNamara was born December 23rd, 1876, and that James Barnabas McNamara was born June 2nd, 1882. There were two other boys, Robert A. and Daniel F. There were two girls also, Alice and Marie.

We found that J. B. McNamara had been sent to a House of Refuge as an incorrigible when he was a boy. Another interesting discovery was made in the search for incidents of his childhood days. His great boyhood friend was named Bryce. J. B.'s mother did the washing for the Bryce family. It was from familiarity with the name Bryce that he chose the alias "J. B. Bryce," when he went to the Coast to destroy the Los Angeles Times. As a boy he had a reputation for evil. He was always in deviltry and was considered a tough one. When the name "J. B. Bryce" began to appear in the papers in connection with the crime at Los Angeles some of his mother's neighbors declared that the Bryce was not the real James Bryce but was Jim McNamara. In time we found the real James Bryce and had him for a witness to show why J. B. McNamara would use this name. Of course we had signatures on hotel registers showing the "J. B. Bryce" we had been seeking and we also had signatures of J. B. McNamara which showed that the same hand wrote both names. We followed the careers of J. J. and J. B. from their birth to the day of their arrest and at no time was there a single chance under the sun of their getting, fairly, any other verdict than guilty from twelve men. Their only hope was bribery and corruption and the intimidation and kidnapping of witnesses. How I fought the crooked plans operated for them while they waited trial will take several subsequent chapters. At present I shall continue with the disclosures of the personal side of the lives of these two prisoners, following, step by step, the downward career of each.

CHAPTER XXXI

JIM McNAMARA LOSES HIS NERVE

The career of J. B. McNamara, the younger of the two brothers, was just the sort of career any of his friends might have predicted for him. Incorrigible in youth, he grew up to be regardless of all decency and law. Physically he was weak and of the tubercular type. He could not stand dissipation and went down under it, lower and lower.

The younger man became a printer and got a smattering of learning, but not enough to help him out of the dregs into which he had quickly dropped. Although a great deal of money was paid to him from the union treasury by his brother he never saved a cent of it or put a cent of it to any other use than buying liquor or the favors of the lowest type of women. Immediately following the destruction of the Times Building and the killing of the twenty-one people who perished through his act, he left Los Angeles for San Francisco and celebrated his terrible act by scattering money about in the lowest of drinking dives, spending it on women of the streets, negro singers and café musicians. He had no conscience, no trace of it. He did have

fear at times when he would sober up and the list
of his crimes would come before his mind's eye.
He had this fear in the woods of Wisconsin after
his pals left him. Once again he had it and he had
it so greatly that he went to pieces. He knew that
the Burns agency had been employed to investigate
the destruction of the Times, but months had gone
by and he had never uncovered a shadow and there
had been no hint that he or his brother was suspected. Still, at times, he would ask himself if it
was not possible that some one was watching him
and that among his drunken friends there was a
spy.

The occasion when J. B.'s nerve gave way completely was when he was in Ballagh, Neb., soon
after the Times disaster. He was met there on a
special trip by a friend from Cumminsville, named
Frank Eckhoff. J. B. was keeping under cover by
order of J. J. until he could connect with McManigal for the trip to the wilds of Wisconsin.

The first day the two were in Ballagh together,
J. B. caved in and asked Eckhoff to kill him. He
was seated in the kitchen of the boarding place, a
Savage automatic gun hanging on his breast from a
strap. He could have slipped the weapon from its
holster and ended his life in a second, but he did
not have the nerve to do it.

"I want you to go out hunting with me and kill
me," he told Eckhoff. "You can say it was acci-
dental and it will be getting me out of this trouble

easily. I KNOW THEY ARE GOING TO GET ME!"

Eckhoff declined to kill him.

J. B. had already told Eckhoff that he and an Anarchist had blown up the Times and had related to him how he had wrenched off the gas pipes so that the smell would give the impression that the explosion was caused by escaping gas.

The days they spent in Nebraska gave J. B. much time for reflection and he saw where he had made many mistakes that should not have been made. He recalled that he had left some laundry in Los Angeles and that it had the initials "J. McN." on it.

"They will get me on that damned laundry," he blurted out one day. "I'll bet there are detectives going around to every laundry shop in the United States to see who that stuff belonged to."

He was not very far off on that conjecture for we did catch up with his laundry with the telltale initials.

The fear of the gallows had crept into the heart of this wholesale murderer. He and Eckhoff were driving in a buggy near Ballagh when an automobile came up behind them. J. B. jumped from the rig and ran and hid under a bridge, trembling. One time he saw Eckhoff smiling and he turned on him savagely and demanded to know if he was going to give him away. Just before reaching Omaha on their way to Cumminsville and the McNamara home, a man came through the coach asking the names of the passengers as he took a straw vote on the coming election. This terrified J. B. for a moment as he thought the man was a detective looking for "J. B. Bryce."

Eckhoff took the dynamiter home and there J. B. met his brother, J. J., and told him about the forgotten laundry. J. J. found J. B.'s remaining handkerchiefs and other linen with initials and turned them over to Eckhoff along with some batteries and bits of fuse, telling him to burn them up so that no one could trace Jim by them. He also gave Eckhoff five alarm clocks to hide. Eckhoff sold them for the price of a few drinks.

Fear was now striking at the heart of J. J. McNamara also. When he was ready to start back to headquarters at Indianapolis he hired Eckhoff to trail him to the Cumminsville station so that he would know whether he was being shadowed. He was being shadowed all right but so skillfully that Eckhoff was unable to uncover the men having him under surveillance. We were using what we call a "long shadow" on J. J.

At the station Eckhoff was paid two dollars by J. J. for this feeble attempt at uncovering our expert shadows.

Eckhoff, who lived near the McNamara home, had known the family for years. He was frequently used both by J. J. and J. B. as an assistant in various jobs and it was Eckhoff to whom J. J. McNamara made the proposition that he place a dress suitcase filled with dynamite and a clock under the seat of a train and blow up his secretary, Miss Dye. This was during Christmas week of 1910. J. J. McNamara had tired of the woman and Miss Dye knew enough about his affairs to have hanged him. That it was a time of peace on earth and good will to men did not lessen the degree of murder in the heart of J. J. McNamara. He wanted the woman blown up in the train and explained to Eckhoff how he could set the clock and leave the train at a station before the explosion. The dynamite would have killed her, wrecked the train and killed many innocent people besides. He was willing to pay Eckhoff $200 for carrying out his orders and was sorry when Eckhoff backed out.

This brings us to the point where we can take up J. J. McNamara's private life as our operatives uncovered it.

CHAPTER XXXII

J. J. McNAMARA AND HIS WOMEN

J. J. McNamara, sometimes described as the brains of the dynamiting crew, the man who was given an annual allowance of $12,000 to be expended as he saw fit for the iron workers during their strike, had more capacity for self-education than his weakling brother. He might have led a useful life and could have advanced from a trade to a profession, for he did pass an examination for admittance to practice law. But he never practiced.

When he was made Secretary-Treasurer of the International Bridge and Structural Iron Workers' Union he found himself in practical control of the money that flowed in from the various locals. The executive board allowed him one thousand dollars a month to pay the expenses attendant on handling the strike from headquarters. He could draw this money in almost any manner he chose, making out checks to cash or to himself.

While Hockin was trimming McManigal and while Eckhoff was selling the little clocks for the price of drinks, and while petty graft and petty theft were in progress on all sides, J. J. McNamara managed to fatten on the hard-earned money of those structural iron workers who did actually work.

Let us look over the list of women on whom he spent good money of the union. While the actual workingman on the job was denying his own wife a new hat or skirt and himself the necessities of life, so that he would keep his union dues paid up, J. J. McNamara was passing along the money to Katherine Kent in Indianapolis. This woman lived in a house kept by a woman known as Minnie Grayson. Katherine Kent was not only a courtesan, but she also turned out to be crooked in other ways, and left Indianapolis after being charged with robbing one of her male admirers. McNamara was Katherine Kent's favorite until she departed the city suddenly in order to avoid a trip to police headquarters.

Then came a very interesting creature of the gentle sex. Her name was Katherine also, and Mc-Namara was devoted to her. She was bright and knowing, and she became deeply interested in labor affairs. She traveled constantly from one coast to the other, visiting many cities where open-shop firms were building. McNamara was putting her to good use in the masked warfare, for she could get information at times without creating any suspicion where a man would have had no chance at all. We had reason to believe that she was on Mc-Namara's pay roll. McNamara was devoted to her, as was another union man, who came to meet her in the course of those affairs which brought the two men together preceding explosions.

Katherine II. had a big wardrobe for the average woman, changing her dress daily, and she always had plenty of money. But as far as outsiders knew she was a woman of no visible means of support. She was full of life and vim, and went on hunting and fishing trips with male friends. She made a number of trips about the country with McNamara. Finally the other union man asked her to marry him. He evidently gave her time to think it over, for she went to a close friend, who afterward became our informant, and sought advice.

"I don't love this man or care for him enough to marry him," she told this friend. "What shall I do?"

"Marry him," advised the friend. "You will have a home, and this will prevent you from becoming a tramp."

The mysterious lady of many country-wide journeyings took the advice. They were married in the summer of 1911, and so she passed from the life of McNamara. She has a home, but at this writing her husband is in a Federal prison, while McNamara is in San Quentin with fourteen years' imprisonment before him.

This woman was not only bright, but she was an exceedingly well versed woman, and with signs of cultivation. In the light of what our operatives learned about her past we had reason to believe that her services came in handy for the McNamara defense just before the trial of the McNamaras was called.

Sometimes detectives for opposing sides in a big case will strike against each other and then there generally comes a real tug of war. Is it possible that it was the vivacious and shrewd Miss Katherine II that caused one of our operatives a great deal of worry in Sonoma, Cal., during November of 1911? Operative No. 25 wrote to Manager O. H. K. at Portland, Ore., for whom he was working, informing him about a strange woman who seemed to be getting in touch with some witnesses he had in his care for us. In his letter he said:

"Now, about this woman, F. B. W., I am puzzled, between you and me. I was to her room to-night for two hours, and I have won her over and jollied her along, but she will not commit herself as to what she is doing or who she is, but she made this remark to me. I said to her, 'I will meet you later perhaps,' and she said with a little laugh, 'But you will get yours before then.' I asked her to explain, but she just laughed. She then said later to me: 'I wish we could be friends; I like you very much,' and I said, 'We can, can't we?' She said, 'I wish it might be so.'

"So you can see that there is something in the wind somewhere. Then she also said, 'Oh, I knew you were coming here; I was looking for you.' Can

you beat that? Oh, it is a nice puzzle, and with
N. W. being sick and ——— and his woman, and
then have something like this turn up. It certainly
has got me jumping. But if she gets anything on
me she certainly will have to see me first, as I am
watching her every move.

"I settled our bill for the week last night as I
did not want it to run on. I do not think we will
stay here over a week longer, as it is pretty expensive, but I will have to have more money before
next week. With kind regards and best wishes, I
remain,

"Faithfully yours,
"J. M. F.

"Cash balance on hand to date, $35.75.
"No Time:
"No expense:
"Reported
"Portland, 11-10-11."

Incidentally, we had a bright little lady working
for us also on the Coast during the summer before
the trial. How simple and yet how disarming are
the methods of capable women detectives may be
shown in one task she performed for us. She was
known as Operative C. M., and her "subject" was
stopping in the Hotel Manx, San Francisco. Her
duty was to find out just who this man was. He
was going under the name of Kelly. She was also
to find out the number of his room and report to
the San Francisco manager.

Here is the way she performed the task:

"Investigator C. M. reports as follows:

"Acting under instructions of Manager W. A. M., at 6 p. m., I telephoned to the Hotel Manx, and asked for Mr. Kelly. I was immediately connected with a room, and a male voice answered. I said, 'What room is this?' and the voice answered, '532.' Then I said, 'That is the wrong number,' and hung up.

"I then proceeded to the Hotel Manx, accompanied by investigator H. M. I left him on Powell Street, in front of the hotel, went into the hotel, and took the elevator to the fifth floor. I proceeded to room 532, and knocked on the door. While I stood there waiting for an answer a man who I know to be 'Larry Sullivan' walked up behind me, and said, 'Who are you looking for?' I replied that I was looking for a young lady who had sent word that she would be at the Hotel Manx this afternoon. He said, 'Well, you have the wrong room. This is my room,' and attempted to become quite friendly with me. I assumed the part of an embarrassed girl, and said I would go to the office, and see if I had made a mistake in the hotel. 'Sullivan' accompanied me to the office, and assisted me in attempting to locate my friend.

"At the desk I asked for Miss Genevieve Van Hulfen, and, of course, was told that she was not there.

"I then left the hotel, walked north on Powell

Street to Geary, east on Geary to Stockton, south on Stockton to O'Farrell, west on O'Farrell to Powell, where I met Investigator H. M.

"I gave Investigator H. M. the number of Sullivan's room, and returned to the office at 7 p. m., at which time I discontinued.

"No expense.

"Time: one-half day.

"————— —————.

"Reported S. F.,
   "July 29th, 1911."

CHAPTER XXXIII

THE TRAGEDY OF MARY DYE

When Katherine II was disposed of, J. J. Mc-Namara turned his charms toward a young woman he employed as a stenographer. Her name was Mary Dye, and she was from an Ohio town.

Miss Dye was a quick and efficient worker, and employer and employee got along famously together. As they became more intimate the formalities faded away, and the secretary-treasurer of the International Union and the stenographer called each other by their first names. Miss Dye finally got to know just about as much as anyone in the labor councils knew as to what was going on. J. J. McNamara first realized the danger of this when she opened his mail one day and found in one of his letters a clipping telling about a dynamiting.

"Oh, Joe!" exclaimed Miss Dye from her desk, "what do you think? They have blown up that scab job." She held up the clipping and shook it.

It was then that McNamara got frightened. He had gone too far with the girl to drop her suddenly and she knew everything. He had paid her various and considerable sums of money. There was only one safe way, and that was to kill her. The

Christmas week following this incident of the clipping she was to visit her parents in Ohio. McNamara gave her the Christmas-week holiday and then
tried to get J. B., his brother, or Eckhoff, to put
a bomb under her seat in the train and blow her
to fragments. There might have been more brutal
crimes contemplated by other fiends in history, but
this proposition struck me as being about as fiendish
as any I had ever read or heard of.

Miss Dye started out with a reputation as a good
and hard-working girl.

In 1909 Miss Dye lived with modesty and strict
economy in the Bertha Ballard Home for Working
Girls, No. 411 North Delaware Street, Indianapolis. One of the aims of the people back of the
Home is to protect the working girl from influences
that would be harmful for her. A girl enjoying the
privileges of the Home would have to bear a good
reputation.

Miss Dye was bright and made friends. Her
conduct seemed all that it should be, and she set
forth to get employment in Indianapolis. She was
both stenographer and bookkeeper, and knew her
business thoroughly. She had little trouble finding a position, but her whole life might have been
changed for the better had she landed in any other
office than the one she did. J. J. McNamara employed her, and she took up her duties in the office
of the International Union.

It is not any sport to hit a man when he is down

—if you consider J. J. McNamara worthy of any sympathetic consideration; but the man who was really knocked down and out in this masked war was not the head dynamiter, but the honest working-man in the craft of iron worker, the man with a wife and children, a job and a decent method of living. The honest iron worker was robbed of his money for years by the spenders and murderers he trusted as officers of his union, and his organization was set back a good twenty-five years by the exposures that followed their arrests and conviction. No honest worker will enjoy reading the story of Mary Dye.

We learned from the lady in charge of the Home for Working Girls that Miss Dye lived there for about eighteen months during 1909 and 1910. After she secured employment at union headquarters McNamara called on her at the Home and was received by her just as other girls received their men friends. So far everything was fair and open and above board. Soon the other girls heard from Miss Dye that she was engaged to McNamara. She called him "Mac," and it looked as if another romance was shaping in the Home.

The matron, a Miss Hyatt, informed us in our investigation that McNamara's intentions seemed to be of the best. She and the girls in the Home had every reason to believe them so, especially after McNamara sent his mother, one of his sisters and a brother to visit the girl in the Home.

If J. J. McNamara was really in love with this girl it seems inconceivable that the affair should end as it did. If this manner of approach to her was designed to bring about her betrayal then the man's heart was about as black as it is possible for a human to carry in his breast. McNamara's people visited Miss Dye more than once, and this served to wipe out any possibility of suspicion on the part of the matron and the girl's chums.

Miss Dye could be trusted, under the circumstances, and so when she absented herself from the Home for days at a time nothing was thought of it. She did really visit Mrs. McNamara in Cumminsville, but at other times she was away on trips with the secretary-treasurer of the International. She explained that her duties compelled her to visit different cities and she told Miss Hyatt at various times incidents that happened when she was away. These incidents showed how faithful the girl was to her lover. She told Miss Hyatt on one occasion that when she was in Cleveland McNamara met President Ryan at the depot by telegraphic appointment. Miss Dye went with him to meet Ryan and stood off at a distance. The two labor men got in conversation and she noticed two men who managed to get close to them. Her suspicions were aroused and she watched them until she felt certain that they were detectives. Then she went to McNamara and told him that he was being watched.

On another occasion Miss Dye told Miss Hyatt

that she had received a note asking her to come to police headquarters in Indianapolis. This was in January or February, 1910. It is probable that at this time McNamara was getting a little tired of the girl, but the girl was still staunch and faithful. The Indianapolis detectives, she told Miss Hyatt, made her an offer of $5,000 cash for a certain letter in McNamara's files. They offered to give her this money if she got the letter to headquarters for only a half hour. They promised its safe return to her and she could replace it in the files of the union's secretary-treasurer. She refused the offer.

Employer and employee were now living a life which required frequent explanations on the part of the girl if she was to remain in the Home and pass as an unmarried woman. To some of her friends she said that she was married to the labor man, and she showed some of them the picture of a baby boy which she said was her son. To Miss Hyatt she said that the picture was that of her little brother. Finally she withdrew from the Home and took a room at No. 207 North Street, where McNamara had a room. During this time McNamara had been pretty lavish with the union's funds and had given Miss Dye $300 in a lump sum at one time, quite a cash gift for a working girl.

In the North Street house just the sort of complication that would be caused by a man of McNamara's caliber came about. He had exerted his charms to win the landlady, and he won her. She was in love with him, very much in love with him, we learned from other lodgers. So when Miss Dye came to the house this "heart-breaking" dynamiter had two ladies hanging at his heels. Hockin, Jim McNamara and other men visited J. J. in this house, and they would remain there for days at a time when there was anything important afoot. When McNamara was out of town, on one of his trips, he would send letters and postcards to the lovesick landlady daily.

J. J. managed to keep the two women apart for some time, but his room connected with that occupied by Miss Dye, and the landlady became jealous. There was a scene between the women, and Miss Dye was ordered from the house. She went away, but returned later and showed the landlady what she said was a marriage certificate, telling her that she and J. J. had been married in Cincinnati.

McNamara now wanted to get rid of Miss Dye, but she hung on. He had plenty of the union's money to pay her, but she wanted something other than money. She had given him everything a woman could give a man and was now being cast into the discard. McNamara finally froze out the girl. To get rid of her he kept his office closed for a month, only using it in the night time.

Miss Dye was without a job and without her lover. She became acquainted with a man named Meyers, and McNamara heard of this. This knowledge promised him a means of getting rid of the girl for all time. He sent word to Cummins-ville for Frank Eckhoff, his odd-jobs man, to come to Indianapolis. We secured an affidavit backed by evidence from Eckhoff which gave us the story of how McNamara, by the most heartless means, finally got rid of the girl.

"J. J. told me when I reached headquarters," swore Eckhoff, "that he wanted me to shadow Miss Dye and a man named Meyers. He described her to me and told me what kind of clothes she wore so that I could pick her out. He said that she seemed to be able to spot every other man he sent to shadow her, and explained to me that as I was short she would not find it so easy to spot me. I had seen Miss Dye a number of times, as he had brought her to his mother's home in Quarry Street, Cumminsville.

"After receiving J. J.'s instruction I went out, and at 11 o'clock at night I picked up Miss Dye standing on a street corner with the man named Meyers. They went to the Hotel Morton, and I followed them. They registered under their right names and took separate rooms. Then I went over to J. J.'s office and told him where the two were stopping. Hockin then went over to the hotel and found out what floor they had their rooms on. He got a room for me on the same floor.

"I went to the room under the name of 'Willis' and took a position where I could watch them that night. I remained the next day and night, watching them.

"Miss Dye and Meyers went to a show the second night, and when they returned they both went to Miss Dye's room. I called up J. J., who was waiting in his office at union headquarters, and told him. He said for me to stay there and watch, which I did. Then I called him up again. He told me to come over to his office and I went. Hockin, J. J. and I then went over to the hotel together. Hockin got a boy to take a fake telegram to Miss Dye's room, and when she opened the door J. J. pushed his way in.

"Meyers was not there. She was alone.

"J. J. remained in her room talking, and then came to my room, where Hockin and I were waiting. He did not tell us what Miss Dye had said, but he said practically that she would not bother him any more. He told me that he wanted to get her on a charge of blackmail. He said he had given her $300 on account of one child, and that she wanted $300 more, claiming that he was the father of another child. He said that it was for this reason that he wanted to catch her with Meyers. J. J. and Hockin left, and I remained in the hotel. I heard Miss Dye making a complaint that there was a man in room 60 who was spotting her, and so I got out and found a room elsewhere. J. J. gave me five dollars cash for this work and paid my expenses."

That ends the romance of Miss Dye of Marietta, Ohio.

J. J. McNamara having failed to bring about her murder, murdered what reputation she had left after he had finished with her.

CHAPTER XXXIV

THE STORY OF THE ODD-JOBS MAN

The most careful of criminals will leave an opening for their detection at some time or other. For five years of the masked war the McNamaras and their fellow conspirators covered their work very well. But their success became their undoing. They became brazen and careless. In the handling of Frank Eckhoff, the odd-jobs man, both the McNamaras were so disregardful of their own interests that in the end they gave him to us as one of our most important witnesses.

Eckhoff was a weak brother, content with small jobs and small pay, and not used to large sums. He was no two-hundred-dollar man, as was J. B. McNamara or McManigal. Fifty dollars was a large sum to him.

After the arrests of the McNamaras and McManigal we heard of the intimate friendship between J. B. McNamara and a Cumminsville man. All that we knew was that the man's name was Frank, and that he lived in Cincinnati somewhere. I sent operatives to that city to find this one "Frank" from the many other "Franks" there.

Of course, by elimination, we got down to only those men having Frank for a first name and who were known to the McNamara family. We finally got Frank Eckhoff. Agents for the McNamaras had reached him ahead of us, but they had done the work of boys. They got him to sign a statement that he had never helped the McNamaras blow up any places or was paid money by them to do any work of that sort.

Such a statement was useless to the defense. We went after him and finally prevailed on him to tell everything that he knew. We got a sworn affidavit from him, and we had a witness who would fully back up the McManigal confession and drive home the charges against the prisoners. But Eckhoff had already given a statement to the effect that he knew nothing against the two men, and we could not tell when he would turn around and repudiate his affidavit. To avoid any influences that the defense would start to bring about such a change we proceeded to isolate Mr. Eckhoff. He disappeared. Two of our operatives also disappeared. Only the two operatives, myself and Raymond Burns, knew where he was. The defense searched high and low for him, but there was to be no capture of this prisoner by them. We were running no chance of having him rushed away as Mrs. Caplan was rushed away. Our operatives kept moving about the country with Eckhoff, all the time getting from him everything that he could recall in addition to

what he had put in his affidavit. They went from
town to town, leaving no tracks behind them, but
always keeping in touch with me. And as they did
this we had operatives going over all the ground
opened up by Eckhoff's affidavit and verifying every
word of his sworn statement just as we had verified
the confession of McManigal.

Eliminating the information given us by him concerning J. J. McNamara and Miss Dye, already related, Eckhoff's sworn statement of his share in the
masked war was as follows:

"Frank Eckhoff, being duly sworn, deposes and
says:

"That I resided on Kentucky Avenue in Cumminsville, Ohio, with my parents for eight years previous to February 28th, 1911, on which date I was
married and moved to my present address, 4168
Hamilton Avenue, Cumminsville, Ohio.

"That I have been acquainted with J. J. McNamara, J. B. McNamara and Robert McNamara
and their family for the past eight years. I am particularly well acquainted with J. B. who is fa-
miliarly known to me as Jim. We loafed together
a great deal about the corners in the vicinity already described and some time in the year 1908,
J. B. McNamara asked me if I wanted to make
$50. I told him I did, and asked him what he
wanted me to do. He replied evasively by saying
that it was a matter in the interest of the unions,

and that he wanted me to blow up some iron work that was being erected by a non-union firm, the Riter-Conley Company, the particular job that he wanted me to blow up being on Sargent Street, Cincinnati. I accompanied him to the place and looked over the situation. He told me that it would be an easy matter to carry the dynamite down there and set it off, and if anybody was in the neighborhood I needn't lay it down, but could bring it back. I told him that I was afraid to do this. A day or two later I saw in the newspapers that this place had been dynamited, and while J. B. did not tell me so, I was sure in my own mind that he had done the trick.

"Some time subsequent to this, in the winter of 1910, he asked me to take a trip with him to Pittsburg, which I did. We registered at the St. Charles Hotel in Pittsburg. I do not know what name he put down, but I registered under my own name. The next day, after lunch, we took a train to Beaver Falls, got off and walked out and looked over the Beaver Falls bridge, which J. B. told me was being erected by the McClintic-Marshall Company. He pointed out the place and said, 'That is the job we want to blow up.'

"Then we walked to Rochester, and he conducted me to an old vacant building on the outskirts of the town, near the river. We went in the basement of this place, and he got a shovel which he had hidden in under the rafters and dug up some earth, then lifted a board and showed me three cans of stuff, which he said was nitroglycerin. Then he went to another corner of the building where he dug another can up. He took the stopper out of this can, smelled it, and said that it was still frozen. Then he replaced all four cans where he had found them. He told me he was going to use this stuff on the Beaver Falls bridge.

"At the time he wanted me to carry the stuff down and blow up the Cincinnati job, he explained that there was a clockwork attachment, and I would have plenty of time to set it down and get away as it wouldn't go off; if I did not set it down there would be time for me to get back to him and he could disconnect it.

"We walked from Rochester back to Beaver, got the train, and returned to Pittsburg. That night he left me at Pittsburg, and said he was going down to look over the job. He returned later and said that the place was so well guarded that it was impossible to get by the watchmen. We kept our room at the St. Charles Hotel two days and a night while we were making the trip down to Rochester. Then he sent me back home and stayed there himself.

"When he came back from Pittsburg he didn't say anything about the Beaver Falls job or any other jobs for a long time. He came to me and asked me if I wanted to do some work for him around his house, grading and moving stone, and I went to work for him."

Eckhoff here swore to the share he played in the freezing out of Mary Dye by J. J. McNamara and Hockin. He went to Cincinnati after finishing the job of shadowing Miss Dye. His affidavit then goes on as follows:

"I loafed around for a time. J. B. was also there in Cincinnati, and one day he told me that J. J. might want me to go to Pittsburg for him in a few days, and I said I would. In the meantime Jim went out of town—I don't know where he went. A couple of days later I got a letter from J. J., which I burned, containing a money order in my name, payable at Cincinnati for $25. I think this was in April or May, 1910. In the letter he stated that he wanted me to go to Pittsburg and look up Miss Dye at her address, 509 Holland Avenue, out in the suburbs. I shadowed the house long enough to find out that Meyers and Miss Dye were living together at the address given, and then wrote J. J. from Pittsburg to this effect. His instructions had been to stay only a few days, so when I had written him I went back to Cincinnati.

"I saw J. J. the following Sunday in Cincinnati, and he asked me how much money I had left. I told him only $7, and he said he would give Jim some money for me. When I saw Jim he gave me $3, which made $10 and my expenses for this work. While I was in Pittsburg on this trip I stopped at a boarding house in Williamsburg, but don't re-

member the name. Think I could tell the house if
I saw it.

"I knocked around Cincinnati without any regular job during the summer and fall. I think it was
a few weeks after I saw the accounts of the Los Angeles explosion in the papers, when J. J. called me
up one day on the long distance 'phone at the saloon
on the corner near where I lived, Fred Haus' saloon,
at Colerain and Lieber Avenues. He, J. J., called
up three or four times during the day and as I was
away each time, finally left word with either Haus
or my sister that I should come to Indianapolis. I
went to Indianapolis that night on a late train about
eleven o'clock. Got to Indianapolis early the next
morning and called J. J. up about eleven o'clock.
He told me to come to the office, which I did. He
then asked me if I wanted to make a trip to Nebraska for him. He never told me what had happened
but told me he wanted me to go out there and tell
Jim to get away from there. He said he didn't think
Jim was there yet and that I would probably get
there about a day later than Jim. He told me to
tell Jim to go to work somewhere; that it didn't
make a damn bit of difference how much he got for
the work. He gave me $75 in cash for the trip.
I went with him to a bank near his office where he
got the money, which he handed me in the bank.

"I took the Monon from Indianapolis to Chicago,
the Northwestern to Omaha, changed trains there,
and bought a ticket for O'Neil, Neb. Had to stay

at O'Neil that night and stopped at a little place near the station where I registered under my right name, I think from Omaha. I went to a livery stable that night and tried to get a team but had to wait until the next morning for one. The next morning, about 6:30 or 7 o'clock, a man drove me to Chambers, about 22 miles; and from there I had to hire another team to take me down to Ballagh, about 14 miles more. I arrived there around 4 or 5 o'clock that afternoon. Jim and Jim's mother and his brother-in-law and his sister, Alice, were there. The family saw the rig coming and came out to meet me. Jim did not come out. I found him sitting on a bed in the house, cleaning a shotgun. He was surprised to see me and said he thought it was Joe. We took a walk outside and he asked me what was the matter. He said, 'I guess Joe sent you out,' and asked me if he was coming. I told him no, and told him that Joe wanted him to leave there as soon as possible and go to Sioux City, Iowa, or any other little town and go to work; that J. J. said to suit himself about where he wanted to go and that he didn't have to worry about the money as J. J. would send some to him when he needed it. He looked kind of down-hearted and said to his mother, 'I'm in trouble, Mum.' She asked him what the matter was and he replied, 'Oh, just a little trouble; I have got to leave to-morrow.' His mother seemed to be worried about it, and when she got me away from the others asked me quietly what the trouble was. I told her I didn't know, but that J. J. had sent me out. I stayed there that night. We, J. B. and I, got up early the next morning, about 4 o'clock, and Howard Knabb hitched up and drove us to O'Neil, about 40 miles. We got there about half past two in the afternoon, and had lunch at a restaurant there. Got a train from there at about 4 o'clock for Omaha, and from there came on back to Chicago, where we checked our suitcases at the depot and waited until nighttime to get a train for Indianapolis.

"When we left Ballagh, J. B. was wearing a brown slouch felt hat, a brown suit that looked new but was badly wrinkled and hadn't been pressed, and, I think, black shoes. He told me that he had bought this suit on a jump and asked me how I liked it. After we got on the train he put on a pair of spectacles and wore them all the way back to Indianapolis. I had never seen him wear glasses before.

"We reached Indianapolis the next morning. I called up J. J. at his office and told him I was back and that J. B. came back with me. Then while J. B. waited at the depot, I went up to J. J.'s office. I told him where J. B. was and how he was dressed —he asked me about that. J. J. told me to have J. B. meet him on the corner of some street, up near the Court House and Washington and that he, J. J., would drive by there with a horse and buggy and take J. B. for a drive. J. J. got the rig at

Wood's Livery Stable and met J. B. at the place designated. They said they were going for a drive out in the country and expected to be back about 11 o'clock that morning. I was to call him up when they got back, but I called up about 11 o'clock and as they were not there I took the train for Cincinnati about 12 o'clock. I had already been given $17 (the amount I had left after taking out my expenses) which J. J. told me I could keep for my trouble.

"While we were at Ballagh, J. B. told me that he had come back from the west to Chicago and then had gone from Chicago out to Ballagh. He did not tell me anything he had done, but from everything I knew, I was under the impression that he was keeping under cover on account of the Los Angeles matter. That was one reason why I left Indianapolis and got back to Cincinnati as soon as I could.

"Some time after my trip out West, I wrote a letter to J. J. asking him to loan me $20 and received a reply stating that he didn't have it. Subsequent to this, Bob McNamara called at my house and said that Jim was in town again and wanted me to meet him at 5th Street and Central Avenue, Cincinnati. I was kind of 'leary' about it as I didn't know what he wanted; but I went down and met him and we had supper together. He asked me if I had ever asked J. J. for work and I told him no, but that I had asked him to lend me $20. He said that J. J. had told him about that, and that J. J. didn't have the money or he would have given it to me. J. B. asked me if I had any money and he gave me $5. Then he asked me to pay for the supper, which I did. He came back to Cumminsville with me and went to his own home and I went to mine. J. B. only stayed a few days and then left but didn't say where he was going.

"About three weeks after that I wrote again to J. J. and asked him to lend me $25. He wrote me a letter, refusing again.

"Just before his arrest, I wrote to J. J. again and said that if he didn't send me the money that I asked for that I would turn over to the other side and get it and said I wanted $50. He sent me a telegram (Postal) signing his own name, I think, which read: 'I am sending you a letter in to-day's mail.' This was addressed to me at my house. On the following Thursday, I got a letter with a money order for $50 in it. The letter said, 'I am lending you $50 and will talk matters over with you when I see you again in Cincinnati.' The Saturday night after that, he was arrested.

"After his arrest, about four weeks later, I think, I wrote to Hockin and asked for $125. He never answered my letter and I didn't hear anything from him until Bob McNamara came to me and said Hockin told him I wanted $125 and asked him what I wanted it for. I told Bob that I had it coming to me—that they owed it to me (which they didn't). And Bob said the lawyers up there said that they could do what they wanted to me on a charge of blackmail; and that Hockin had said if I was starving to death he would give me a few dollars out of his own pocket. I told Bob to tell Hockin that I wasn't starving to death.

"Then, after that, I wrote Mr. Burns anonymously, telling him to reply to George Williams, General Delivery, but I never went to the General Delivery to ask for a letter.

"I neglected to state that previous to asking for the $125, Bob McNamara came to me and said that two lawyers wanted to see me down town. I went down with Bob—he told me not to let anybody know about it—and he introduced me to Keegan and Harrington at the Hotel Haviland. They got my statement and asked me whether I had ever seen McNamara with any dynamite, whether I ever carried any for him or saw him making any bombs and whether I had any letters from him. I told them 'no' to every question, but every statement I made to them was false. I signed the statement but did not swear to it.

"Right after I made this statement, Detectives Shafer, Ball and McDevitt of the Cincinnati Police Department called at my house. I told them I didn't know anything. I lied to them for the purpose of shielding McNamara and also omitted to tell them anything about the statement to Harrington.

"Then Detective Shafer and Charles F. Trotter of the Burns Agency called on me and took me down to headquarters, where they asked me about my employers. I voluntarily made a statement to them of my own free will, without any urging on the part of the police officials. I told them the whole story from beginning to end, and they asked me to come to Indianapolis and I volunteered to accompany them.

"Shortly after his trip to Rochester, J. B. Mc-Namara sent me to Cincinnati to purchase ½ dozen dry cell batteries No. 5. I purchased these at some electrical supply store on 4th Street near Plum, and I think they had red wrappings. Some young man waited on me. They cost 15 or 25 or 30 cents apiece.

"At different times I also bought for him about ½ dozen gallon cans like painters have. I bought them at Ira D. Washburn's place on Central Avenue near Court Street, Cincinnati. He always wanted corks with them. He didn't tell me what he wanted them for.

"Just before the Cincinnati explosion, I was at the home of J. B. one day and he took me up on the hill near his home and said he had some nitro-glycerin hidden there and wanted to look at it. He found three quart bottles filled with nitroglycerin hidden alongside of a log. He smelled of it and said it wasn't very strong and then poured it out on the ground and broke the bottles. He thought there were four quarts there but he could only find three.

"J. B. always told me in a joking way that he wanted the batteries for the door bells up at the house. In speaking of nitroglycerin, J. B. referred to it at least once as 'soup.' He said that was what the cracksmen called it.

"Just after the explosion in October and before I went to Ballagh, J. J. gave me four clocks one night in Cincinnati and told me to keep them for him. They were small repeating alarm clocks with the name 'Junior Tattoo' on the front of them and were made by the New Haven Clock Company. J. J. said that he wanted these clocks again, but I was broke, and with a young man named McEvoy, who lives on Whittier Street, we sold the four clocks to the following parties:

1 to Robert Eckel, locksmith, at 4464 (?) Hamilton Avenue, near Chase, for 60c.
1 to a saloon keeper at the Keller House, Colerain and Hoffman Streets, for 50c.
2 at Elmore and Spring Grove Avenues; one to a saloon keeper and one to a man in the place; got about $1 for these two.

"At the same time that J. J. McNamara gave me the clocks he also gave me a couple of handkerchiefs and several pairs of cuffs and told me to burn them up, which I did. He also gave me a piece of fuse with powder in it, about half a roll, which I cut in pieces and burned.

"(Signed) Frank Eckhoff.

"Subscribed and sworn to before me this 7th day of November, 1911.

"William S. Garber, Notary Public."

CHAPTER XXXV

DEATH THREATS TO WITNESSES

From the time of the arrests of the McNamaras and McManigal until December 1st, 1911, when the two brothers confessed their guilt in court in Los Angeles, my agency never for a second relaxed its efforts to make good their case and also get in readiness the material that would aid the United States Government in prosecuting the labor men who had joined in the dynamite conspiracy.

Every possible effort to beat us out was made by the agents for the defense. Threats of murder were openly made to witnesses, evidence was manufactured or destroyed, plans were laid to kill me, as I have told before, my offices were broken into and searched, bribes were offered my men and the veniremen drawn for the jury. One man, employed by counsel for the defense, was caught red-handed bribing a juror the day before the McNamaras pleaded guilty. Detective Biddinger, traveling from Chicago to Los Angeles with important documentary evidence, was offered a large sum of money if he would permit himself to be hit over the head and the evidence taken from him.

All the while there was one long and bitter roar against me. I was accused of planting the dynamite, General Otis was accused of engaging in a frame-up and mass meetings were held all over the country where money was raised for the defense and where the flame of hate against Capital was fanned.

As early as June, 1911, we learned that Tveitmoe, the "Old Man" of the Pacific Coast, was planning to get a spy from the defense within our own ranks. We provided him with one, Investigator E. W. McK. On the 9th of June a representative of Tveitmoe approached our man. He explained that the "Old Man" was very anxious to be put wise to the inside methods of Burns. He also wanted to get information as to how I had successfully landed the guilty men in the land fraud cases in Oregon. He said that Tveitmoe was out of the city but that he (our man) would hear from him on his return. Tveitmoe's agent gave our man the information that efforts were being made to have a general strike of all the unions in the country so that on the day the trial started not a wheel would turn or a hammer be heard in the whole land.

My operative took in everything that was said to him. Tveitmoe's man explained that gas had caused the Times explosion and that the defense would prove it. The defense would prove that the men employed on the paper had been complaining of escaping gas for two weeks and that the very families that had been bereft of their wage-earners would swear to this. The widows and children of the murdered men would testify, he said, that the men who were killed had complained of the escaping gas. He said also that there were union men employed by the Times and that they would aid in the defense by giving testimony to prove that gas had caused the destruction of the plant and the loss of twenty-one lives.

But the first and most desperate move, declared the informant who thought that he was getting next to one of my men to betray our plans, was to bring a halt to all industry and thus frighten the jury and the judge and all concerned. Money was pouring in for the defense and Darrow and his aides had all that they could ask for.

Besides threatening to murder our witnesses if they persisted in telling the truth, the agents for the accused men hired two assassins and paid them in advance to kill District Attorney Fredericks and General Otis, the owner of the Times, if a verdict was brought in against the McNamaras. The plan or idea was, perhaps, that this double killing would frighten the successor to the district attorney and that a half-hearted fight would be made against an appeal.

The man who gave us the information about the hiring of the gunmen was John Love, a prosperous business man, mine owner and courageous citizen of Denver. Mr. Love said that while on a trip to

Colorado Springs, October 16th, he sat behind two men in a coach. From their conversation he made out that they had met in Denver and were on their way to attend the McNamara trial in Los Angeles. They had a bottle of whiskey, which they used frequently and their voices rose in conversation. One of them had come over the Rock Island and the other over the Burlington to Denver. He could not help but hear all of their talk. When one of the men turned he saw a button of the Workmen of the World on his lapel.

One of the men told the other that he had been given $1,000 while the other said he had been given $500. For this money they were to kill Fredericks and Otis if the case went against the McNamaras. An old Englishwoman on her way to the Coast was sitting opposite Mr. Love. She heard the talk of the two gunmen and leaned over to Mr. Love and asked him if he thought that the men would murder two people in cold blood for money.

Mr. Love was exceedingly anxious to avoid any notoriety but his sense of duty was such that he gave the information. He described both men to our operatives. The man who got the $1,000 wore his hair long, his neck was unshaven and his brow was receding. The other man pulled out his wallet to prove that he had received his five hundred dollars and counted it on his knee. Mr. Love saw this done and saw that some of the bills were fifty dollar certificates.

This will sound as pretty desperate business and some people who are comfortably remote from the underworld may even question it or say it is too much like a dime novel. But we had every reason to believe that assassins were easily hired in this case.

Desperadoes do not belong to any one section of the country or to any one period of time. These two gunmen were of the same stamp as J. J., who was a product of existence to-day. It is easy to believe that J. J. would have stopped at nothing after his endeavor to have Miss Dye, his cast-off sweetheart, killed with dynamite. We learned from McManigal in Los Angeles jail that he was even more desperate as an outlaw than his known crimes gave him discredit for being. McManigal informed us that McNamara had become so bold with his power of ambush that he was planning to become a highway robber on a great scale so that he could supply himself with more money for keeping up his fight.

"It's a good thing you've got J. J. in here," said McManigal to Operative McLaren, soon after they were locked up, "for he told me that he was keeping tabs on an Indianapolis bank messenger who carried large sums of money daily. He was planning to hold him up and had already picked out a man to assist him. He also planned to hold up the box office on the day of the big automobile races. He figured that there would be close to $100,000 in cash in the box office. He had planned to have J.

B. assist him in this hold-up. He said, 'We need the money.' "

And now we come to one of the most brazen of the attempts to save the McNamaras by intimidating my witnesses. That business was meant when a murder threat was passed this particular witness I had every reason to believe. The witness was a very important one and so I handled this detail myself in person.

CHAPTER XXXVI

EFFORTS TO BUY OFF WITNESSES

In the first half of August prior to the trial of the McNamaras I was engaged in going over with District Attorney Fredericks the matters under investigation as I received the reports of my managers and operatives. There were many important things to watch and always the crooked work that was going on in behalf of the prisoners. We had many special investigations in progress besides the regular work of my force and one of these investigations took me away from Los Angeles to San Francisco. In the latter city I learned that Tveitmoe and his associates were so violent in their denunciations of me that a most vicious feeling obtained against me. I was advised to be extremely careful and to take every means to protect myself from attack. I took what precautions I considered sensible and when my operative reported to me the sinister statement of a certain distinguished member of the California bar that the only thing that could save the McNamaras was my withdrawal from the case I returned that gentleman my compliments with the information that he would be killed immediately the news was given out that I had been assassinated. This brought immediate relief. Then I went to the office of Fremont Older, editor of the San Francisco Evening Bulletin. This paper had done a great deal to create hate against me personally. I talked with Mr. Older about that and all I could get from him was that he was taking the side of the "under dog." I made a special, confidential report to District Attorney Fredericks which might have become matters of court record had I been killed during the trial.

After a week-end at the ranch of Mr. Rudolph Spreckles, in Sonoma County, I returned to San Francisco and was informed that our witness, G. H. Phillips, of Oakland, who would positively identify J. B. McNamara as "Bryce," the man who purchased the dynamite for the Times explosion, had been approached and that his life had been threatened. It was night when I got this information, but I hurried to Oakland and the home of Mr. Phillips. I was unable to get any answer at the door, and thinking that the family might be away paying social calls, I kept the place under surveillance. We watched until 12:30, when it was evident that the family was within but was afraid to answer any summons at the door. I remained in Oakland the rest of the night and resumed my personal investigation the next morning, August 24th.

At 9 a. m. I again called at Mr. Phillips' residence and found Mrs. Phillips, who informed me that her husband was being threatened by the defense; that he was at the Giant Powder Works and only came home on Saturday nights. She stated that while she felt a little nervous over the matter, she was proud of the stand her husband was taking, viz., that he would not permit anybody to frighten him out of doing what he considered his duty as a good citizen. I then left, secured an automobile, and went to the Giant Powder Works where I met Mr. Phillips. He stated that he proposed to stand pat and no amount of threats would frighten him out of doing his duty, but admitted that he felt a little nervous over the situation; he said, however, that he would be firm in his stand to do what was right.

He further stated that about a month ago two men called on a Mrs. Hyde, a friend of Mrs. Phillips, who lives on Myrtle Street, between 12th and 14th, Oakland. They asked her in regard to Mr. Phillips and wanted to know what kind of a man he was; whether he did not have a deaf and dumb child; whether she had ever heard Phillips discuss the McNamara case with Mr. Hyde. They stated they were detectives and represented the defense. Mr. Phillips further stated that on Wednesday, August 9th, a friend of his called on him (Mr. Phillips) and said he would like to talk to him in confidence. At this point I desire to state that Mr. Phillips declined to furnish the name or address of this person, but in discussing the details of the case he inadvertently mentioned the name of "Patsy" and also inadvertently disclosed that he was at the Mare Island Navy Yard. When his attention was called to this and he was shown how easily Patsy could be located, he gave me the name of Patrick Gilmore. He stated that Patsy (as he called him) called upon him and stated that he had been approached by a couple of parties who requested him to go and see him (Phillips) and get him to change his testimony, or rather, his identification of James B. McNamara by saying that the man he saw he remembered distinctly had a scar on his neck, or something of that sort; and told him that he could name his own price. Phillips declined to do as they requested and said he would have nothing whatever to do with them.

Patsy also informed Mr. Phillips that a Mr. Hitchcock called, and that later a man and woman, whom Patsy did not know, called at the Mare Island Navy Yard and wanted to see him concerning this same matter. Mr. Phillips stated that this detective who called on Patsy had also called on Mr. William Flynn, the packing foreman at the Giant Powder Works, while Flynn was at the Winchester Hotel in San Francisco. On Saturday, August 19th, Mr. Finkleday, of the Giant Powder Company, called Mr. Phillips to the 'phone and told him the San Francisco office of the Giant Powder Company was on the 'phone. Mr. Phillips went to the 'phone and found the party at the other end was Michael Gilmore, a clerk in the office of the Giant Powder Company. Gilmore said, "I want to come over and see you to-night," meaning to his home at 1312 Market Street, Oakland.

Gilmore called that night and said, "I came to warn you that a man named Kelly called on me with a letter from a priest who is an old friend of mine, and Kelly stated he was a relative of the McNamaras and wanted him (Phillips) to meet Gilmore; he asked if Gilmore could come over and see him (Phillips); Kelly asked him to change his testimony as to the identification of McNamara and to say that the man he saw at the Powder Works had a finger off. Phillips asked Gilmore who this man was and Gilmore replied that he had asked Kelly what his business was and Kelly stated he was a mining man and banker. He also asked Kelly if he had sent anyone else to see Phillips and he said yes, that he had sent word to Phillips through William Flynn. Gilmore informed Phillips that Kelly stated this was the last time he would send for him and that if Phillips went to Los Angeles and testified he (Phillips) would suffer an awful death.

Gilmore said he was to meet this fellow at Solari's restaurant that night and take dinner with him. He also told Gilmore to tell Phillips he could name his own price. Phillips told Gilmore to tell those men to go plumb to hell, that no amount of money would purchase his testimony and that he could not be frightened. Phillips also stated that there were

two men who had called at a saloon up near the
Powder Works, and from the descriptions I am
satisfied who they were. They were inquiring about
Mr. Phillips and his habits and associations.

Mr. Phillips also reminded me that at the time
I called upon him at the Powder Works in October
last he had informed me that he heard Schmitty
call one of the men (the little fellow) Dave—
meaning Dave Caplan—and that J. B. McNamara
was smooth-faced at that time, while he now has
a mustache.

Mr. Phillips then introduced me to William
Flynn, the packing foreman at the Giant Powder
Works, who stated that on July 23rd, while he was
at the Winchester Hotel, 76 Third Street, San Francisco, about 6:30 or 7 p. m., two men called and
gave the names of Sullivan and Harrington. Sullivan asked Flynn to go to his room, and on reaching
there he told Flynn that they were friends of Mc-
Namara and asked if he was a good friend of
George Phillips. Also asked Flynn if he knew a
man named Gilmore who worked up there. Flynn
told him Gilmore formerly worked at Giant, Cal.,
but that he was now at the Mare Island Navy Yard.
They then asked him if he ever heard Phillips talk
about his identification of McNamara; he replied
that he had not. They asked a number of questions
about Phillips and his habits, and when leaving they
said, "Now, if you can't do us any good don't do
us any harm," and, shaking his finger at Flynn,

asked him not to say anything about their visit. Harrington informed Flynn he was from Chicago and Sullivan said he was from Los Angeles. He described them as follows:

Harrington—Age 50, height about 5 feet 7½ inches, weight 170 to 180, short, wears glasses, glasses in two pieces.

Sullivan—50 years, 5 feet 11 inches or 6 feet, born in London, Canada, weight about 200 pounds or more, smooth face, black derby hat, dark suit.

Flynn says a man shadowed him around San Francisco for two days. Flynn remembered that when they were leaving Sullivan said, "Remember, everything said to-night dies here; if not, look out." Harrington said to Flynn, "They have no evidence against the McNamaras; they are just trying to job them." They wanted to know from Flynn if Phillips was a church member, and if he did not have a child, and then tried to show an intimate knowledge by asking if he did not have a deaf and dumb child, a girl. He said that he had been at the works looking for Flynn and was informed he was at the Winchester Hotel in San Francisco. The man giving the name of Harrington showed Flynn an envelope of a telegram on which was written the name Harrington.

After leaving Phillips I returned to San Francisco and immediately called at the office of the Giant Powder Company in the Mills Building and found Michael Gilmore, who is apparently a very fine young fellow. He is bright and intelligent and has been connected with this concern for a number of years; occupies a very responsible clerical position.

At first Gilmore declined to discuss the matter with me or to have anything to say about it, and it took the very hardest kind of pounding to get him to discuss the matter at all, as he stated he didn't want to be drawn into it or connected with it in any way, and that he would have had nothing whatever to do with the case had it not been for the fact that the man named Kelly, who called upon him, had threatened the life of Mr. Phillips. That was his only reason for going over there. This I do not believe; I think he was persuaded to go over by the parties who called on him. Finally, Mr. Gilmore admitted that on Saturday, the 19th of August, a man called on him with a letter from a Catholic priest and after showing him the letter stated that he was a friend of the McNamaras and that he wanted to get Mr. Gilmore to see Phillips and urge him (Phillips) to change his identification of J. B. McNamara by stating that the man he saw at the Powder Works in October had the index finger missing from one hand, or something of that sort; that Phillips could name his own price and that Kelly would give the money to Gilmore to pay it to Phillips. His exact language was "Phillips can name his own price and the money will be handed him by you." Kelly further stated that he

(Gilmore) was the last man who would be sent to Phillips and that if he did not comply with their request, but persisted in testifying against the Mc-Namaras at Los Angeles, he (Phillips) would not die a natural death. He further stated that the testimony of Phillips would hang the two Mc-Namaras.

After considerable persuasion I induced Gilmore to let me see the letter written by the priest, which he had in his pocket, and it read as follows:

"My dear Michael:
"I wish you would assist this man in the information which he will need. Help him in every way you can. Mr. L. M. Kelly will explain when he sees you."

After another long wrangle Gilmore permitted me to see the name signed to the letter and I communicated this to Fredericks in person, as I promised Gilmore I would not put it in the report, and it is only because of that promise that I am not putting it in here. I felt that every man connected with this case—priest or no priest—should be called before the Grand Jury and made to tell all he knew about it.

Gilmore was very badly scared and trembled all during our conversation; he was very much agitated. He then informed me that he had an appointment with this same man to take dinner with him **that** night. I then had Gilmore come down to the door of the Mills Building, where I had two of our men take a look at him so as to be able to identify him when he met Kelly. I was satisfied from the description given by Gilmore that L. M. Kelly is L. M. Sullivan.

I then sent operatives Reed and Spaulding to cover the Hotel Manx, where Gilmore was to meet Kelly. Gilmore, as agreed upon, went to the Manx Hotel at 5:45 p. m. and met Larry Sullivan in the lobby of the hotel. They then proceeded to the Heidelberg Inn at Ellis Street near Market, entering there at 5:55 p. m. Sullivan returned to his hotel at 7:45 and at 7:55 talked with the telephone operator and did some telephoning, then went upstairs in the elevator.

As the reader will recall we later positively identified "Kelly" as "Larry" Sullivan with the aid of the woman detective.

CHAPTER XXXVII

HOW EVIDENCE WAS DESTROYED

In these days of constant exposure of corruption it was a highly encouraging and satisfying feeling we experienced when I had finished the investigation of the Phillips incident and could report to District Attorney Fredericks that our witness was neither to be bought nor to be frightened. If he was to meet a "horrible death," as he was told he would by the McNamara agents, he would not flicker before the possibility of it being meted out to him. His splendid wife was with him in his stand and I was indeed grateful to them both during these trying moments of intrigue, trickery and threatened assassination just prior to the trial.

Mr. Phillips could positively identify J. B. McNamara as "J. B. Bryce" and he would so identify him if he lived to reach the witness stand.

There was never an end to the efforts to cheat justice until we finally cornered the defense with the bribery of a juror and Clarence Darrow threw up his hands, his two clients pleading guilty.

In Peoria, Ill., our investigators sought to get the hotel register with the signature of "McGraw"

—McManigal—and we found that some one had reached the register first and had cut out the pages which we wanted. Our men did not give up, however, for in this Peoria hotel McManigal had left his wallet with over $400 under his pillow and an honest woman employee had found it and had turned it into the proprietor. The woman had gone away and had married, but we traced her and showed her a picture of McManigal and she identified it as a picture of the man who had left the money in his room. She fixed the date approximately. By her we could prove that he was in the hotel at the time he said he was and we had the mutilated register to offer in evidence.

A woman witness we had in Indianapolis in the triple explosion and fire which destroyed construction work, stable and garage of the contractor, Von Spreckelsen, in 1909, was approached by a union printer who offered to run away with her, give her a deed to his house and lot in Indianapolis and provide her with all the money she wanted to spend. We had an operative living in the same flat with this woman and he managed to keep her steady and she did not succumb to the bribes. Moreover, she became interested in the effort to bring the dynamiters to justice and did some excellent detective work for us.

The defense was eminently successful with Mrs. McManigal, however, and she sold out after trimming us and trimming her husband.

After going over to the defense, Mrs. McManigal got fifty dollars from our Chicago office to take her to Los Angeles and when she reached Los Angeles calmly turned us down and worked so hard to influence her husband in prison to go back on his confession that at times we were fearful that she would succeed.

McManigal was half crazy to see his wife and to hear from his children. She had tortured him with messages of her illness and with a long period in which she did not write him a line to let him know whether she and the children were with food and shelter. McManigal wrote her imploring letters. He knew that his only chance to save himself was in making good with evidence for the State and she could have made good for him by telling the truth. She knew J. B. McNamara and J. J. They had both been to her house in Chicago. She knew J. B. both as "Bryce" and "Sullivan" and she knew every detail of the business her husband was engaged in. In her flat J. B. had made up a number of infernal machines with batteries and clocks and on one winter's evening she had seen him and her husband thaw out frozen dynamite on the radiator while the children played about them!

As black as was the record of McManigal, he was turning State's evidence as much for the sake of his wife and children, whom he sincerely loved, as he was in the hope of saving his own neck. When he learned that his wife had gone back on him he was first puzzled, then frightened and then horrified.

The man was crazy to see her and the children and when she arrived in Los Angeles we took steps to bring this about. On June 27th, 1911, we arranged with Assistant District Attorney Ford to have Mrs. McManigal taken before the Grand Jury at 10:30 a. m. We were to take her husband into a small room adjoining the grand jury room and have the two meet there. When McManigal was told of this plan he cried, "My God, yes, take me to her right now. Let me talk with her." Operative McLaren, who was his body guard in prison, told him that he would have to wait until the arrangements were completed. McManigal became hysterical and would laugh one moment and cry the next. He kept crying, "Oh, my darling wife, you will not go back on me."

"She has got to help me," he told McLaren. "She knows all. She knew that Hockin cheated me out of $75 on every explosion I pulled off for him until he owed me $450. She knew every time I went away on a job and many a time I told her I did not know whether I would come back as I might be killed by a watchman or blown up with my own dynamite. She knows everything and she has got to help me."

As we were soon to learn, Mrs. McManigal's task was to whip her husband around for the defense and she kept at it to the very end. She was aided by George Behm, McManigal's uncle, of whom he had been very fond as a boy and a young man. The defense had secured the aid of these two.

The meeting between husband and wife in the room adjoining the grand jury room occurred that day. After they had talked for a while McManigal called in Operative McLaren and urged his wife to talk with him for his sake and for her own. She turned on McManigal with a curt, "You shut up!" and when McLaren tried to induce her to aid her husband she stuck her fingers in her ears. She doubled her fist in her husband's face and finally fell in a faint. She was unconscious for an hour and a half and a physician was summoned. When she came to she asked for Darrow. Darrow and the other lawyers for the defense were outside. McLaren opened the door and told Darrow that Mrs. McManigal wanted to be taken home. The lawyers were furious and Darrow shouted, "How long are you going to keep up this outrage?"

"You had better get an automobile for the lady," was McLaren's reply.

The long fainting spell did not seem to have any lasting ill effect on Mrs. McManigal. Under the direction of the lawyers for the defense she began her campaign to take her husband away from the prosecution. One would think that ordinarily a witness would be safe in jail, but McManigal was not. He was reached more than once and the story of how the defense worked to break him down will make a series of chapters perhaps unequalled in any story of fact concerning the administration of justice in this or any other country.

A less alert man than McLaren would have seen his charge taken from him and McManigal would have turned from his first resolution to tell the truth and the whole truth and our chief witness would have been stolen from us.

Mrs. McManigal managed to inform herself, or be informed, when McLaren left the prison to attend to certain work that required his attention. Although orders had been given to allow the prisoner to see no one without McLaren being present there were certain outside political influences at work and Mrs. McManigal managed to get into her husband's cell with him alone and begin her task of winning him away from us. McLaren heard about it from an informant in the jail and hurried there. He found Mrs. McManigal gay and cheerful as she left her husband's cell and met Attorney Job Harriman in the corridor. She had made a good start. McManigal was weakening. McLaren hurried into the cell and McManigal told him that they had not discussed the case. McLaren knew that he was lying and finally got out of him that Mrs. McManigal had gotten him to sign a request asking Darrow and his associates to call to see him as his attorneys.

After talking with Mr. Harriman, Mrs. McManigal asked to see her husband again and she was permitted to talk with him in the visitors' room for ten minutes. Things looked very bad. McManigal had weakened terribly. His wife, it seemed, had done the work she was sent to do.

We had to start all over with McManigal to convince him that he had everything to lose and nothing to gain if he gave in to the urgings of the defense. Now, although McManigal was tight in the hands of the law, a prisoner and a confessed dynamiter and the most important witness for the State, counsel for the defense managed to have him reached time and again by means so subtle that even J. J. McNamara, himself a prisoner in a distant part of the jail, managed to get messages to him.

We were compelled to double our own guard on McManigal and to equip a dictagraph in his cell unbeknown to him.

CHAPTER XXXVIII

MCMANIGAL NEARLY DRIVEN CRAZY

Mrs. McManigal proved a veritable thorn in the side of the prosecution. We had her constantly under shadow and found that she was frequently being coached in her campaign to get her husband to go back on his confession and aid in the acquittal of the two McNamaras.

Despite our efforts to have a witness present when Mrs. McManigal talked with her husband in his cell, the influence of her attorneys was such that she was given all the leeway possible to swing her husband the way they wanted him swung. The dictagraph, however, aided us and with it and the constant questioning of McManigal by McLaren we found out all that transpired during these visits.

The prisoner's wife coaxed and urged. She told him that the McNamara attorneys had told her that if he would call them in as his counsel they would see that he was freed and that he got a good job. They could even give him an appointment in the very jail where he was incarcerated. She told him that the lawyers promised to provide for them for life—for the whole family—and that she would be given several thousand dollars in cash besides.

The offering was a tempting one, especially when the children were included and Mrs. McManigal assured him that the agreement would include provision for them as long as they lived. McManigal, loving his wife and loving his children, thought seriously of the proposition and did, as I have related heretofore, sign a request for the calling in of Darrow and his associates as his counsel. But after we had convinced him that this was not the thing to do and he had recalled the request he was never again tempted to sign another. When he got his nerve, finally, he realized that he was in a most precarious position, that his confession had been carefully checked up and that it would be a simple matter for the defense to throw the whole mass of crime on his shoulders and send him to death.

McLaren found his prison charge very much excited after one of these visits of Mrs. McManigal. It was then that he was realizing that he might be offered as the human sacrifice to save the McNamaras.

"Go ahead, Mac," advised McLaren, "and tell me all about it."

McManigal then told him of the tempting offers and exclaimed: "I'm next to the whole business! I told her that they did not want to get me free and provide for me and my family, but that they wanted to hang me. I told her that they would do it if she did not come over to my side and back me up in my stand."

McManigal then said that his wife had told him that his uncle, George Behm, was on his way from Portage, Wis., to see him. We knew what this meant. McManigal was fond of this uncle and the uncle was to be added to the force that would try to win McManigal away from the prosecution.

There were many days of genuine agony for McManigal as he sat in his cell, his heart hungry for the sight of his little boy and girl and the love of his wife, who was drifting farther and farther away from him and working with those who meant him no good. He, a big, strong man, who had thought nothing of putting his life in peril time and again as he dodged armed watchmen to set off infernal machines, would sit and sob like a child at times.

"I was happy with my wife and children and contented with the money I was making in my trade," he told McLaren one day. "Then the two McNamaras and Hockin got hold of me and gradually forced me into the dynamiting business. I could look my wife and children in the face after a day of honest work. I had no trouble on my mind until they got me to go in with them to dynamite the non-union shops. After that my life was a hell on earth. Now my wife and innocent children are disgraced."

He was moaning and sobbing bitterly as he talked with my operative. He said that once he had done a job the McNamaras had him where he had to take orders.

At times McManigal would rage against the Mc-

Namara brothers as the cause of all his trouble. He told McLaren that he would be satisfied if he were given a club and turned loose on the two of them. With his heavy frame and the big scar on his forehead, he looked as if he could carry out his wish to kill the two of them and end the whole business in that way.

The confessed dynamiter was constantly tortured despite the care we took to hold him steady and keep his mind in a reasonable state of calm. His wife, for a long time before her arrival in Los Angeles, had not answered his letters and when she had answered them it was to tell him that she was very ill and that the children of neighbors had jeered at his little boy and girl, stories that worked him into a frenzy. From the very first, even when she calmly collected fifty dollars from my Chicago office to proceed to Los Angeles, she was working for the McNamaras and their lawyers. McManigal had been double-crossed all along the line and would have been sent to the gallows if he had given in to the pleadings of his wife. He had been robbed of a part of the money paid for his work as a dynamiter, he had been relieved of what he had left by his wife—down to his stickpin—and after being put in jail he was in a fair way of being made the goat for the whole business.

There were influences inside of the Los Angeles jail that we had to watch. For a time McManigal had a cellmate whose attorney was also one of the

lawyers for the McNamara defense. We feared
that this prisoner might try to pump McManigal
and serve as a spy for the McNamara camp. Mc-
Manigal was also reached by J. J. McNamara
through a prisoner known as "Happy," who was a
trusty and could communicate between cells. Finally our man was changed to another cell, but it
was a dark basement cell, and McManigal was ten
times more miserable there. His health became
poor and McLaren worried greatly about him.
The McNamaras were allowed pillows, cushions
and other things for comfort, and finally McLaren
made a fight for his charge and got him back to a
cell where he could get some sunshine. Daily we
had McLaren talk with him in an effort to keep his
mind relieved of the things that were worrying
him so greatly. McLaren brought him papers,
fruit and cigars and saw him morning, afternoon,
and night. Of course the purpose was as much
to keep him under surveillance in his cell as to hold
him steady to the prosecution's side.

The wife having failed to turn McManigal to
the defense, the uncle, George Behm, was then
brought to Los Angeles and thrown into the breach.
As a boy McManigal had just grown up by himself.
Among the few people that had been kind to him
was this uncle and he remembered him with genuine
affection. His own father, in whose barn at Tiffin,
Ohio, Ortie had made a dynamite caché, had done
nothing to aid him in his plight. His own wife had

turned against him. The man wanted some blood
tie to turn to and when he learned that this friendly
uncle was on his way he cheered up. He would
have some one he could talk to, some one he could
hope to find encouragement in.

There was nothing promising to us, however, in
the coming of this uncle, for the lawyers for the
defense had roped him and Uncle George was being
brought to Los Angeles to help the McNamaras
and not his nephew.

CHAPTER XXXIX

WORSE THAN ANY THIRD DEGREE

How McManigal's uncle was used against him is best told in the report written by McLaren and turned in to Manager Mills of the Los Angeles headquarters of our agency on Thursday, June 29th, 1911. His report is as follows:

"Inv. M. McL. reports:

"At 8.00 a. m., I arrived at the Agency when Manager E. R. M. and I discussed the many different angles the case has assumed in the last few days. Plans were made to meet the situation fully.

"Leaving the office at 10:30 a. m. with Manager E. R. M., we went to the County Jail to see Mc-Manigal. Before going up to see Mac, I talked with Jailer Gallagher. He told me that Ortie had acted something awful this morning. It seems that Ortie's uncle, George Behm, passed on the opposite side of the street from the jail and Ortie saw him from the jail window. Ortie pounded on the wire screen, and called at the top of his voice, 'Oh, Uncle George, here I am. Oh, come up, and see me, Uncle George.' In a hysterical way, Ortie kept this up until quite a crowd had gathered in front of the jail.

"Gallagher had to go up and lock Mac in a cell away from the window. Gallagher said that Mac acted like a crazy man. He also said that Uncle George did not come to the jail to see Mac. I will here state that Ortie's uncle arrived in Los Angeles yesterday and was with Mrs. Manigal at the Job Harriman apartments last night.

"Ortie is in a very nervous condition bordering on a collapse. The tactics the attorneys for the defense are using, look to me as if they were trying to unbalance Mac's mind. First, they have turned his wife against him; second, they have refused to bring his children to see him; third, they have paraded his uncle past the jail where they knew Mac would see him, and up to this writing, twelve o'clock midnight, his uncle has not called upon him. This last was a bitter blow to Ortie. This uncle had practically been a father to him, he having lived with him a great deal in his younger days.

"The last few days Mac has been telling me how much he thought of Uncle George, and many times he said, 'He will not go back on me.'

"After Gallagher had told me of the Uncle George affair, I went up and saw Ortie. I advised him and pleaded with him to try and control himself. I told him that every move and action of his was watched by 'trusties' in the jail and everything he did or said was being carried to J. J. I told him how his actions of this morning would be grabbed by the defense attorneys. They would say he was insane or anything else to discredit him. He said, 'I know it, I know it, but my God, they are torturing me.' Mac told me that he had not slept for five nights, and before leaving I saw Jailer Gallagher, and requested him to have the doctor give Mac something to make him sleep."

This third degree work from the sidewalk was kept up for some time, the trips of the uncle being timed carefully so that McManigal would be at the window. McLaren had a task on his hands convincing his charge that these trips were designed to break him down and that he could expect nothing from his relative.

When we got McLaren's report of how this scheme worked we lost no time in getting ready for any charge by the defense that McManigal was irresponsible. He had acted like a crazy man at the window and we knew that the lawyers for the defense had been fully informed of this. We looked into the future and laid plans to offset any contention that McManigal was mentally defective. We sent operatives to his home town and among relatives and friends who could give accounts as witnesses of his actions since childhood. We looked up his company officers when he was in the army and through them we could prove that he was not mentally defective but was sound in mind and body when he was enlisted in the Ohio regiment during the Spanish War.

We were always ready for emergencies, always looking into the future and at no time did we leave a single man engaged in the defense of the Mc-Namaras unshadowed. We had an operative waiting on the restaurant table where these gentlemen gathered for lunch, we had operatives always keeping Tveitmoe and his associates under surveillance, we had operatives watching Mrs. McManigal and Uncle George all the time and then we had the quiet but efficient dictagraph working at cell windows in the jail.

We had trouble making Uncle George answer questions before the Grand Jury after he did finally visit his nephew, McManigal, but we made him answer after charging him with contempt. When he was finally brought around the relative from Portage, Wis., was amazed and stunned when he found the District Attorney asking him about things only he and McManigal had spoken of in the latter's cell. He had not heard of the dictagraph.

It will probably give E. A. Clancy, one of "Old Man" Tveitmoe's chief labor allies on the Coast, a feeling otherwise than that of gratification to know how well he was watched during those days preceding the trial, for it was Clancy who shouted approval to a toast to the McNamaras offered by one of my men.

Operative No. 36 had the job of keeping tabs

on the San Francisco Labor Council. His report of July 9th, 1911, will undoubtedly interest Mr. Clancy and his friends. It is as follows:

"Continuing on operation this morning at 8 :30 a. m., I took the 9:00 a. m. boat for Sausalito. Arriving at Sausalito I took the train to Fairfax Park, Marine County. This park was selected by the International Association of Bridge and Structural Iron Workers comprising the following locals: No. 31, No. 77, No. 78, of San Francisco, and No. 117 of Oakland. All of the most prominent members of the locals were present.

"P. H. McCarthy, with President Joe Sullivan, of the Police Commission, were conspicuous figures. McCarthy asked the gatekeeper how many tickets had been sold at the gate, and he said about five hundred and about twelve hundred more had been taken in, making about seventeen hundred. Johanson and E. B. Morton got on the train when we got to Corte Madera, and when we arrived at the park, we met E. A. Clancy of No. 78 and Dan Cameron of No. 77, Paul Reiner of No. 117 Oakland and R. W. Smith of No. 31.

"We were at the bar drinking when P. H. McCarthy and Sullivan arrived, and after a few moments, Clancy said to P. H. McCarthy: 'Well, if J. J. McNamara had have been here to-day, these grounds would not have held the crowd.' P. H. McCarthy replied, 'No, but if you people think I would stand for anything like that, why you must be crazy. Why, in the first place, the Sheriff of Los Angeles would not take any such chances, and I certainly would not ask the Governor to intercede.'

"Clancy replied, 'His presence here would have shown the people here in San Francisco though that we had some manhood left in our organization yet.'

"Dan Cameron of No. 77 replied, 'Oh, we don't care what the people think, it is what we think.'

"Johanson said, 'Well, they are only trying McNamara for murder. Who are they going to arrest for the destruction of the Times Building?'

"P. H. McCarthy said, 'Oh, just wait, the watch dogs are in hiding just now, but you will hear them barking again soon.'

"Morton said, 'Well, they hounded Mrs. Caplan all over Frisco and came out to my house, but I don't think they will come again in a hurry. I don't think that she has either had a letter or heard from him. She has always been a lady in my house and I will always stand by her.'

"I proposed a toast to the McNamara brothers, and Clancy replied, 'Good for you, old horse; you are right.' P. H. McCarthy said he would go over and see the ladies. Dan Cameron said, 'Well, if it was a carpenter that was in trouble, he would be different, but Mac has always given us the worst of it on every deal.'

"At this time, E. B. Morton asked me to come and have a little lunch. We went down to a table occupied by Mrs. Anton Johanson, where we had a bottle of beer and sandwiches. Mrs. Johanson said, it seemed good to have Anton home during the day as he had to be in Brother O. A. Tveitmoe's office so much since he was away.

"Morton said, 'Well, he is working for a good cause. There will come a time when Anton will be recognized by the union men more than he is now.'

"At this time, 6:00 p. m., Johanson and Morton decided to go home, so I rode down with them to Corte Madero, where they left the train and I returned to the city.

"I discontinued at 7:30 p. m.

"Reported L. A.

"July 10, 1911."

CHAPTER XL

THE ORGANIZATION EXPOSED

During the summer of 1911 all the resources of my agency were used in making a case for the prosecution that would stand any test that the money and brains of the defense might give it. I gave my entire attention to running down every bit of information secured by my operatives and daily made out lists of assignments for the men working on the case. As they investigated and sent in their reports by wire and by mail we would sift the wheat from the chaff and add new witnesses, new affidavits and new exhibits to our gradually growing mass of evidence.

It was reasonable to believe that the biggest effort of the defense would be to save J. J. McNamara, the secretary-treasurer of the union. We had his weakling brother, J. B., tight in the grip of the law and it must have been conceded that there was no hope for him whatever. As matters turned out, finally, the defense was perfectly willing to let J. B. plead guilty and go to the gallows if by doing this J. J. could be saved. It was far from our intention to have any such finale to the case, for J. J. Mc-

Namara was the more dangerous man of the two
and had been the brains and directing force of the
union in its war against society. It was by his word
that the business agents of the union gathered Anarchists and others to send them on their way of
destruction of life and property and it was through
him that the money was paid for the committing
of crimes which made this warfare assume the pro-
portions of a revolution.

Not a day passed from the time of the arrests of
the McNamaras and McManigal that Operative
McLaren did not work with the prisoner who had
turned informer. We had McManigal's confession,
but I knew that gradually he would recall things in
his career as a dynamiter which might help us in
securing new evidence. Each day McLaren would
turn the conversation gradually to dynamiting and
McManigal would begin to talk about some phase
or incident of the war he had participated in. Every
word of information thus received from the prisoner
was embodied in a report at the end of the day and,
regardless of time, distance, or expense, operatives
were made to go back over the trail of the dynamiters to get evidence verifying McManigal's statements.

In this way we learned that J. J. McNamara had
not been above lugging nitroglycerin around the
country himself. Just prior to starting for the convention of the International Union held at Rochester, N. Y., in September, 1910, J. J. packed a

ten-quart can of the explosive in a box made for carrying purposes and another ten-quart can in a telescope valise at headquarters in Indianapolis. He called in McManigal and the two took the "Big Four" train for Cleveland. In the Ohio city they went to the Forest City Hotel, taking the nitroglycerin as part of their hand baggage. They registered and later in the day, by appointment, J. J. met Business Agent Smith of the union on the street and passed him the twenty quarts of explosive. McManigal saw the transfer. J. J. then went East to the convention and McManigal returned to Indianapolis where he cashed a check for $250 given him by his chief. We ran this out quickly, finding the hotel register in Cleveland and tracing the record of the check transaction. Afterward we got Smith along with the other conspirators who were tried in the United States court at Indianapolis.

The convention was in progress in Rochester when the Los Angeles horror was perpetrated and the atrocities of the masked war reached the climax with the murder of twenty-one innocent men. Among the union leaders there was Clancy of San Francisco. Of course, Clancy knew of the plot to destroy the building of the Times, but, it seems, he had not expected such a terrific result. It was during one of the conversations between McLaren and McManigal in the Los Angeles prison that the latter recalled a conversation with J. B. McNamara concerning Mr. Clancy.

"In talking with Ortie McManigal to-day," reported McLaren, "he recalled a conversation with J. B. McNamara while they were hiding in the Wisconsin woods after the Times explosion. J. B. said that when he blew up the Times Clancy was attending the convention at Rochester. He read of the explosion in the newspapers and immediately sent word to an ironworker known as 'Shorty,' who lives in San Francisco, to go to his (Clancy's) house and clean up, meaning by this to destroy everything that would show his connection with the dynamiting that was being done throughout the country.

"McManigal said that J. B. laughed heartily when he told of the scramble by 'Shorty' and Clancy's wife to get rid of everything incriminating in the house."

It is probable that J. J. McNamara and his fellow conspirators felt that their presence in convention in Rochester, N. Y., at the time of the Los Angeles explosion would serve as a sign and good evidence to the world that the Structural Iron Workers' representatives had nothing to do with this dreadful crime. They were all assembled in orderly and parliamentary meeting in a city thousands of miles away. The convention had paid a tribute to J. J. McNamara. His work as the secretary-treasurer was lauded and the progress of the strike was considered satisfactory. The fact that the great majority of the executive council of the union knew of and participated in the war against the employers was not suspected by the public generally. The alarm clock scheme of setting off explosions always permitted the agents of the union to establish alibis for each explosion and in this instance the men directing the wholesale murder in Los Angeles had arranged all the plans before starting East.

One would think that with a spark of humanity left in the hearts of these men they would have given pause when it became known that the destruction of the Times had entailed the sacrifice of the lives of so many innocent people, all working men and all heads of families. The accounts of the anguish of the widows and children as they flocked to the smouldering ruins of the building in Los Angeles to claim the burned and battered bodies of husbands and fathers might have stirred them uneasily, any normal being might believe. No pity, regret or horror moved them.

J. J. McNamara returned to Indianapolis. Olaf Tveitmoe, the "Old Man" of the Pacific Coast, to whom J. B. had reported for his murderous assignment and who supplied the two Anarchists, Caplan and Schmidt, to him as assistants, immediately went into the conference with J. J. He urged that other dynamiting follow the Los Angeles horror. He told J. J. that it would never do to let them stop on the Pacific Coast. "We must keep up the big noise," he told J. J., "so that the authorities will think that the explosions are local and are not directed from headquarters. If there are more ex-

plosions on the Pacific Coast they will never think
of looking in the East for those responsible."

It was this argument that induced J. J. to sum-
mon McManigal to Indianapolis as soon as he
reached headquarters and order him to go to Los
Angeles and try to blow up the auxiliary plant of
the Times and the Llewellyn Iron Works.

McManigal told us that he protested against
going at that time, for the whole country was
alarmed and horror stricken.

"Well," replied J. J., "you have got to go out
there and make a big noise. Look at the chances
J. B. ran. Now if you go out there and get these
two places it will throw suspicion from him."

J. J., Tveitmoe and the rest of the conspirators
had long used the scheme of setting off explosions
at the same time in widely distant parts of the
country so as to puzzle the authorities and make
them confine their investigations to different locali-
ties and they thought that the plan would continue
to work successfully. They did not know that we
had the telltale clockwork bombs that had failed to
explode, the one found at East Peoria and the other
that we picked up in Los Angeles. We had uncovered their plans of warfare and while the authorities of different cities were busy with futile investigations, each in his own jurisdiction, we were
headed for Indianapolis and gradually closing in on
the main camp.

CHAPTER XLI

EXPECTED "GREAT AND BLOODY WAR"

Pending the trial in Los Angeles, we continued weaving the net about J. J. McNamara stronger and stronger as the summer of 1911 wore on. McLaren practically lived in prison with McManigal, guarding him and protecting him from those influences powerful enough to reach within the jail. He proved a never ending well of information and McLaren's reports kept many of our staff busy all the time.

Circumstantial evidence, when backed by exhibits, always proves powerful before a jury. An exhibit, an inanimate thing, does not offer the defense a chance to exert its power in cross-examination. Inanimate things can't lie or get flustered. There is no color for or against the accused in the evidence given by a mute thing. It stands as cold, bare fact. Thus we built up the case against J. J.

McManigal told McLaren that about June 22nd, 1910, while he was in Detroit with J. B. McNamara, the latter received a general delivery letter from his brother. J. J. had enclosed a receipt for an express package. The package was in the office of the Adams Express Company and it contained three clocks and batteries all made up for the job they had been sent on. This information received, a telegram to an operative in Detroit was all that was necessary to start the work of digging into the records of the express company and corroborating the sending and receiving of this package. We found J. B.'s receipt and the record of the whole transaction from the time the package was given in the care of the company until it was delivered and taken away.

Again, McManigal recalled that on December 7th, 1910, he received a postal money order from J. J. for seventy dollars. McManigal was then at his home in Chicago. He cashed the money order at Graham's Bank on West Madison Street. We traced this documentary evidence easily. On the same day McManigal received a telegram from J. J. telling him to come to Indianapolis and bring his suitcases. There was work for him. The money was for expenses. The message telling him to bring his suitcases plainly meant that he would take a journey with a good supply of ammunition. There was easily-traced sequence in these facts and the directing hand of J. J. McNamara showed all through them in a way that could convince any jury.

We thoroughly uncovered the complicity of the majority of the members of the executive body of the union in the dynamiting war, getting positive evidence that they approved the expenditure of one thousand dollars a month through the hands of J. J. McNamara to those who did the actual work of destruction. The bills were duly audited by a committee and the reports of the dynamiters were made by sending newspaper clippings giving accounts of the various explosions for which the union's officials in Indianapolis had supplied nitroglycerin, dynamite and men to set it off.

We uncovered the trail of J. J. McNamara to Tulsa, Oklahoma, and the man named Kiser, who sold him large quantities of explosive before Mc-Manigal was brought into the circle of conspirators to help J. B. with the major part of the work. J. J. was then going under the name of Clark, an alias he used at different times. Kiser picked his photograph out of a collection of pictures and identified it as the man he had sold the explosive to. Mc-Manigal also had used the name of Clark in shipping empty carrying cases for explosives to him in Indianapolis and we were able to trace these express packages.

The trails of the two McNamaras were from one dynamite and nitroglycerin caché to another and although I had but little time in which to indulge in an attempt at a sociological study of what was unfolding before me, as my men made their reports, it was palpable that the conspirators had brought their activities to a point where at any moment the country might have been plunged into bloody revolution and anarchy.

After his arrest, J. B. McNamara boldly declared to one of the Chicago detectives having him in charge, that it was unfortunate that he had been caught when he was. "If I had not been arrested so soon," he told Detective William S. O'Callaghan, "the working people would have had a chance to live. There will be a great and bloody war between capital and labor."

Certainly it seemed that such a war was shaping, for enough explosives had been cachéd at different times by the McNamaras and their fellow conspirators to have equipped an army for operations against a warring nation. Again, J. B. declared that the destruction of the Los Angeles Times was not such a great matter and that the plan was to destroy the whole city of Los Angeles if the attacks on the union emanating from that city did not cease. The plan of the conspirators was to blow up the water works, lighting plants and public buildings, wrecking the entire community regardless of cost to human life and regardless of the suffering that would come to perfectly innocent, law-abiding people.

The McClintic-Marshall Company, especially hated by the union conspirators, had a contract for the steel work in one of the lock sections of the Panama Canal and McManigal was sounded by J. B. to see whether he would go to the Canal and throw enough dynamite in this particular lock to wreck the great work of national defense. At no time was there the faintest trace of consideration for the rest of the eighty or ninety millions of people making up the citizenship of the United States. From ambush these men, drunk with the power they had acquired through years of successful violence and defiance of the law, were ready to utterly wreck the Republic.

In coping with these hidden enemies of society and the laws of the Republic, the police of the various cities, where the outrages were committed, proved themselves utterly hopeless. Their investigations ended with formal reports detailing a few obvious facts. No trails were opened up and no clues developed. Then, too, the regular police forces of American cities are generally a part of the political machine of the party in office and heretofore the unions have played in politics extensively.

The work my agency undertook was a work which another and one-time famous private detective agency had tried to accomplish and had failed to do anything with. The police had given up trying. During the many years in which I served the United States in the Secret Service I had been fortunate in bringing every problem put before me to a successful conclusion. I had not failed in a single instance. My father had been the police commissioner of Columbus, Ohio, when I was a boy. He had not been appointed by a political boss or by a mayor who owed his election to a machine, but had been elected by the people of the city. I suppose it was through the fact that my father was at the head of a police force and could direct that force intelligently and without political interference that I became interested in the art of detecting criminals. Certain it was that when I began to uncover the conspiracy that brought the Los Angeles climax I realized how tremendous was the task before me and how important it was that the criminals be brought to justice. It was more a duty to the law-abiding people of my country that I should bring these criminals to bay than it was a duty to the authorities of one city or county.

When the trails to the real center of the conspiracy were opened wide and the arrests followed there was poured out for me a wide and bitter stream of hatred and opprobrium. I was pictured as a vicious enemy of the workingman and the arch-conspirator employed in breaking up their organization. And yet at no time was I opposed to organized labor. I have always believed that the organization of labor meant good for the workingman and that through it he was benefited and would be further benefited in the future. I am still of that faith despite the wild attacks that were and are still made against me by men of the type of the Mc-Namaras and others who have things hidden they are afraid of.

CHAPTER XLII

"DOWN WITH DETECTIVE BURNS!"

On the eve of the trial of the McNamaras, Mr. Gompers addressed and inflamed the passions of a great crowd of people in Philadelphia in the Labor Lyceum. The date was October 10th, 1911. I had been plentifully attacked before that and even moving-picture shows had been put on to show the working people how I had "kidnapped" the innocent McNamaras.

In Philadelphia a McNamara parade was held and 15,000 people participated in it. Red fire, red flags and transparencies were carried in the parade and a union of Jewish Garment Makers displayed a big sign reading:

"Down with Detective Burns, the Kidnapper."

At this meeting Gompers raged against the manner of the arrest of the McNamaras, declaring that I had entered a meeting of the executive council of the ironworkers and had lured J. J. to the sidewalk and had then kidnapped him and rushed him across the country to a hostile city for trial. He told pathetically of talking with the two accused men just before coming to Philadelphia and painted them as

302

pure and spotless when, even at that time, there was consideration of the question of trying to save J. J. McNamara by sending his younger brother and his weakling tool to the gallows.

Gompers pictured the two McNamaras as martyrs and declared that the two men were being placed on trial "on charges that we know to be absolutely false."

Now there were plenty of honest workingmen who did believe the McNamaras were innocent, men who did not know how their money had been spent and who did not know of the black characters of the officials they trusted. But if ever there was cheap hypocrisy indulged in it was indulged in by Gompers in these public speeches, made for no other purpose than to aid in the cheating of justice and the foiling of the laws which are intended for the protection of the citizens of the country.

How strangely like a squeak sounds the impassioned outburst of Gompers after the two McNamaras have stood up in court and confessed their crimes in order to escape the gallows.

Here is one of the most widely spread appeals issued by Mr. Gompers during the trial, when money was being raised, so that there would be no dearth of it on the Pacific Coast during those days when witnesses were first offered any sums of money to change their evidence and then threatened with death in horrible forms when they refused to be bribed:

"To All Workers."

——o——

"For right is right, since God is God,
And right the day must win;
To doubt would be disloyalty,
To falter would be sin.

"From Los Angeles last October came the news
that a terrible catastrophe had occurred in that city
—that the Los Angeles Times Building had been
destroyed, with the loss of a number of lives. The
first word spoken, even before the flames had completed their destruction, by the emissaries of the
Los Angeles Times contained positive accusations
that organized labor was responsible for the disaster. Qualifying statements were conspicuous by
their absence. Wide publicity was given, warped
and unsupported allegations against the organized
workmen of the entire country were featured, vast
sums of money were dangled in the faces of un-
scrupulous men to fasten the crime upon some member or members of the trades unions. The National Manufacturers' Association, flanked by the
Erectors' Association, Citizens' Alliances, detective
agencies, and a hostile press brought their every
influence to bear and appropriated every available
circumstance to bulwark and fix in the public mind
a mental attitude that the charges made against
oganized labor had been proven beyond the per-
adventure of a doubt.

"The authors of the charge, after months of intrigue and searching investigations, utterly failed to

substantiate the flamboyant and positive accusations that had been made. The public mind was slowly emerging from the hypnotic spell in which it had been enveloped and mutterings of suspicion began to be heard against the originators of the indictments against labor men. The position of the hostile employers' associations became exceedingly desperate. The Times management, with its years of relentless warfare against humanity, fearing that its Belshazzar feast of organized labor's blood was about to be denied, redoubled its efforts and demanded a sacrifice that its unholy appetite might be appeased, and that some union workmen must be supplied to assuage its unnatural and abnormal hunger.

"The record of events is too well known to make it necessary to recount them in detail. That 'the end justifies the means' became the slogan is patent. With all the forces of greed compactly joined, there began a campaign of vandalism the like of which has never before found lodgment on the pages of our American Republic's history. A prominent member of union labor was selected, J. J. McNamara, and one at whom the finger of suspicion had never before pointed, whose life had been characterized by an uprightness of purpose and loyalty to the cause of labor, and whose activities in every walk had drawn to him the commendation of his fellows.

"To give the stage the proper setting, J. B. Mc-

Namara, the brother, was selected as an associate for sacrifice.

"With intrigue, falsehood, and an utter disregard for all guarantees of law, applying physical force, conniving with faithless officials, the two McNamaras were rushed in feverish haste to the scene of the alleged crime. The rights of these two men had been trampled upon—wilfully, flagrantly, wantonly.

"Every man, even the meanest, under the constitutional guarantees of our country, is entitled to a trial by a jury of his peers, and every man is presumed to be innocent until proven guilty. This far the proceedings had been in violent disregard of those guarantees. The charge had been hurled against organized labor, and two of its members are now before the bar to answer these charges. What is the duty of the men and the women of the organized labor movement? What shall be our course? What effort shall we put forth to see to it that justice shall fairly obtain when methods such as these are used against us?

"Funds must be provided to insure a proper defense, a fair and impartial trial. Eminent counsel have been engaged. Arrangements are proceeding that a proper defense may be made. The great need of the hour is money with which to meet the heavy drains incident to the collection of evidence and other expense, made necessary to cope with the corporate wealth and unlimited means behind the persecutors.

"Every man who is connected with the kidnapping of the McNamaras will be prosecuted to the full limit of the law, and a recurrence of the outrage prevented for all time to come. It is proposed that the interests of organized labor shall be fully protected and punishment meted out to detective agencies that assume to be superior to the law. The rights of the men of labor must and shall be preserved.

"The men of labor, unlike the hostile corporations arrayed against us, have not vast resources of wealth and power, but they are imbued with the spirit of justice and humanity, and are ever ready when necessary to make sacrifice for principle.

"The trial of the McNamaras is set for an early date. In the name of justice and humanity all members of our organization and all friends of justice are urgently requested to contribute as liberally as their abilities will permit. All contributions toward the legal defense of the McNamara cases and for the prosecution of the kidnappers should be transmitted as soon as collected to Frank Morrison, No. 801-809 G street, N. W., Washington, D. C., who will forward a receipt for every contribution received and when the cases have been finally determined a report of the amounts received and by whom donated and the amounts paid out of this fund will be printed and a copy of same sent to every contributor.

"Yours fraternally,
"SAMUEL GOMPERS,
"President A. F. of L.
"FRANK MORRISON, Secretary.
"By order of the McNamara Ways and Means Committee."

CHAPTER XLIII

THE UNION WAS GANG-RIDDEN

There are plenty of high-minded, clean and honest labor leaders and under such men organized labor has flourished and the workingmen have met with full and fair consideration of their demands to employers. I do not believe that the rank and file of labor are willing to stand for such atrocities as are shown in the record I have put down in this book. I do not believe that a man with a job, a craft and a family would put up money to hire wholesale murderers. How many men with wives and children would have stood for the proposition to blow up a heavily loaded passenger train as it crossed a high trestle just to show the people of the United States that the railroads could not use rails made in non-union shops? How many men with a spark of faith in God or with a jot of love for humankind would have contributed the murderer's hire to J. B. McNamara when he crept into that little alley filled with ink and paper under the Los Angeles Times Building; when he wrenched the gas jets from their fixture and when his hand did not hesitate as he laid the bomb and a boy passed him going upstairs to his job in the composing room? Did this drunken and degenerate weakling tool of J. J. McNamara, the elder brother, think that that boy's mother was waiting for him after the night's work and that his wages meant her support and her life, and did the cries of the women and children about the ruins of the building touch his heart for one moment? Not much. Jim McNamara spent his blood money among the lowest type of women in the lowest sections of San Francisco, laughed about his work and his brother, whom Gompers lauded as spotless and noble, fished about for an assassin to slay Mary Dye, to blow her up in a railroad coach even though many innocent people were killed with her.

With the cause of labor in the hands of such men only wreck and ruin is ahead of it for the law prevails in this country and it is going to continue to prevail despite the efforts of men of the Gompers type who have made the unions gang-ridden and lawless. With such men the honest and capable union workingman does not stand a chance even in his own organization. If he rises and tries to elect a delegate to a convention whom he may think will be clean from graft, honest and standing for lawful and decent procedure in getting labor's rights, a wrecking crew will beat him down and throw him out.

As I have said before, there are splendid men at the heads of some of the unions and their names are without stain and their unions have flourished. The head of the Brotherhood of Locomotive Engineers is such a man, and Carter, the head of the Locomotive Firemen, is another. I have never heard that John Mitchell ever countenanced acts such as the McNamaras were guilty of.

In our investigations into the affairs of the International Association of Bridge and Structural Iron Workers, the organization betrayed to the Anarchists by the forty men afterward convicted in the courts, two for murder and thirty-eight for conspiracy, we found how gang-ridden it had become when we talked with a highly intelligent member of the union in New York. This man is the head of a family, the provider for a wife and six children, a man of unusual intelligence and force, a skilled workman and one who has held almost every office of trust in his union. His name is not used because of our promise to him.

For the purposes of this chronicle and to show how gang-ridden his union had become we will call him Johnson. He had been an ironworker for twenty years, a member of the union for fifteen years and for ten years of that time had held various offices in the union.

Johnson's honesty was a proverbial matter with the members of his craft. He was useful to the union therefore, for any amount of money could be safely entrusted to him. But as he was honest in money matters he was honest otherwise and would not handle money for crooks who infested the union. From his account of what happened to him in the union the general public will get a pretty good idea of what the honest workingman goes up against when crookedness prevails in his councils.

"I have never had any use for a crook," he told me, "and there are lots of them in my organizaticn. They put me in charge of moneys, etc., depending on my honesty and loyalty, if I do say it myself, to pass it on without having any of it stick to my fingers even though I knew of its rotten purpose. They elected me to office knowing that I wouldn't squeal and afterward they jobbed me because I came out flat-footed and declared that I wouldn't have anything more to do with the crooks who were sucking the money from the poor devils who could not afford it and making a royal living by their tricks and grafting instincts.

"If this dynamiting business had not come up I would be out of a job to-day, because I knew too much, but since it has been brought out they have sent on from Indianapolis to see what kind of a job I would like. I don't want their jobs. I am working here in New York and am getting five dollars a day. I have a home and a family and I want to be left alone by everybody."

Johnson lived up to his reputation of being no squealer. Try as hard as we could we could get nothing from him save his general and temperate protest against the blood-sucking methods of those

men of his union who made "royal livings" by bleed-
ing the poor devils who could not afford to pay.
Johnson was a fine specimen of American workman,
a man of pride and integrity. He hated a liar, a
thief and a grafter.

"They knew that I was getting ready to make a
holler about the rotten conditions and the rotten
jobs and they tried to get me in a dozen different
ways," he said, relating his union experiences.
"During the time of Sam Parks they blackjacked me
right in the meeting hall as I was leaving after I
had expressed myself and I carry the scar to this
day. I would be willing to tell all that I know, but
if I did my family would suffer and in the end I
would be hounded from pillar to post and I would
not be able to get another job. I would like to see
some of the crooks in the union go to the scaffold—
no, I don't mean that, for I do not believe in capital punishment, but I would like to see them sent
to some island where they could not practice their
rotten methods any more. I could not stand for
anything underhanded or mean and that is why I
did not stand better with that crew, you may believe me or not. When the wrecking crew did me
I told them that some time I would get even and
then, when this dynamiting business began to come
out, they fell over themselves trying to get to me,
fearing that I would carry out the old threat."

Here was one honest and clean workingman who
got the blackjack from the grafting element in the

union. There are plenty of them in every local organization where men of the type of the McNamaras and the rest gain control and misrepresent the cause of labor.

I honestly believe that in the end sincere friends of labor organization will find that the work I did in the uncovering of the masked warfare, with all of its horrors and depths of iniquity, will prove of lasting benefit to their cause. No cause can flourish when grafters lead it and it is my honest belief that the good sense of the American people will always exert itself in dealing with big industrial problems. I believe that the law will never be overridden in this country, for the people themselves make the law and they elect the lawmakers. I believe that the people of the United States will solve their problems with intelligence and that the once threatened savage warfare with torch and dynamite has been proved futile. Anarchy cannot reign in the United States.

CHAPTER XLIV

BURNS REFUSES $1,000 A NIGHT

Despite threats to kill and maim and efforts to bribe, I kept on with the preparation of the case.

In the meantime an indictment was found against me at Indianapolis by the Grand Jury, charging me with having kidnapped J. J. McNamara. About this time, I went to Europe on a very important matter, and while there was advised by cable by my son that an effort was being made to rush my case at Indianapolis and forfeit my bond of $10,000. I was compelled to hurry back and go to Indianapolis.

Immediately after the indictment was found I insisted strongly that I be immediately placed on trial at Indianapolis, as I knew there was not a particle of evidence to sustain the charge. But my attorneys pointed out that a long-drawn-out trial might prevent my presence at Los Angeles, where I would be badly needed.

Strange as it may seem, it required vigorous action on my part to collect a portion of the money due me at Los Angeles for the work I had performed, and of all the rewards aggregating over $20,000, which melted like snow before a summer's sun, I have thus far collected only $5,000 from the County of Los Angeles.

In the month of November, 1911, while attending the National Convention of the American Bankers' Association at New Orleans, the American Federation of Labor was holding its Annual Convention at Atlanta, Ga., and a resolution was passed denouncing the Bankers for having passed a resolution of confidence in me.

Just before the confession of guilt by the McNamaras I was informed by my son Raymond J. Burns that an effort was being made to reach Detective Sergeant Guy Biddinger by the defense. A man by the name of ————— Turner, employed in the Detective Agency of Thomas McGuire, in Chicago, had approached Biddinger and told him there was a chance to get rich, and so on. While Gompers was at Indianapolis, Clarence Darrow was called to Indianapolis, and when interviewed by the newspaper men stated that he knew me and that I had not planted the dynamite, and that I had not framed that case. Notwithstanding this statement from their own counsel, Gompers and others continued to denounce me and charge me with framing up the case.

Then followed a warfare to stifle our witnesses, and an effort was made everywhere, first, to bribe them, then to coerce them and then to murder them. J. B. McNamara was constantly advising his lawyers to get rid of Frank Eckhoff, of Cincinnati, as he was a dangerous witness should I happen to find him.

From the very beginning I contended that the rank and file of organized labor were not cognizant of the action of the McNamaras nor did they endorse their methods, but, like many honest men of organized labor, insisted that such men as McNamara, Tveitmoe, and others were a menace to organized labor and ultimately would destroy it if permitted to carry on their atrocious and reckless lawlessness.

Immediately after the confession of the McNamaras I was approached by a prominent theatrical manager, of New York, who called on me with a contract written up and signed by a prominent banking firm, to insure its being carried out, and offering to pay me Ten Thousand Dollars down and One Thousand a night to deliver lectures, beginning at Boston and ending at San Francisco. When I promptly refused this, the theater manager was astounded, and asked me if I realized what I was doing. My reply was that notwithstanding the fact that I needed the money, and it was the greatest opportunity ever presented me to make that amount of money legitimately, I stated that I did not propose to commercialize my connection with this great case, which had been carried on in the interest and protection of Society, and that what he proposed to pay me a thousand a night for telling I would tell the people of this country, in speeches and otherwise, for nothing. This I have endeavored to carry out to the best of my ability.

In doing this I have denounced Samuel Gompers for having denounced me, but *never* charged that Gompers was part of the dynamite conspiracy. His partisans and jealous detectives and others endeavored to construe what I said to mean that I was charging Gompers with being a part of that conspiracy. All I ever charged was that he was derelict in his duty as head of organized labor in this country. He must have heard of these explosions and of the lawless manner in which many of these efforts for the "closed" shop were being carried out, as the Structural Iron Workers were a part of the American Federation of Labor. He was negligent in his duty in not taking some steps to rid the honest members of organized labor and the great organization of labor from the stigma that must naturally attach to them through the action of the violent members participating in this warfare.

During my long official career as an Officer, I had been called upon to investigate important criminal cases, that ultimately involved men in very high places, and as I had never been a respecter of persons in the investigation of these crimes, I did not hesitate to perform my duty as I saw it.

Therefore, I kept gathering, as enemies, as convictions followed, one after the other, my various investigations, an important group of evil doers, who lost no opportunity to attack me and attempt to destroy my character and reputation. When some leaders of organized labor sought to do this, in an effort to defend the McNamaras, they were joined by this group and all sorts of libelous and malicious articles were written in various publications throughout the country, including such disreputable sheets as the "Seattle Times."

Immediately after the arrest of the McNamaras, General Otis then realized that all of the calumnies uttered against me were baseless, and so stated.

From a long experience in prosecuting crime, and especially since organizing the William J. Burns National Detective Agency, I have been cognizant of the outrageous blackmailing methods pursued by private detectives, and I made up my mind that I would do everything possible to expose this class of lawbreakers and parasites on society. I have openly stated, in many of my public utterances from the platform, that private detectives, as a class, are the greatest lot of crooks that ever went unpunished. I have always insisted that the man who wants to follow this business should first fortify himself with a reputation for honesty and integrity, and then he need not care what the people say about private detectives. There are many of them who cloak themselves with this calling solely for the purpose of "blackmailing" and robbing their clients.

The honest private detectives applaud this statement, and are with me in my effort to give to the business an air of respectability, if that is possible.

CHAPTER XLV

The last and completely unsuccessful attempt to save the two McNamaras with the money that had been raised for the defense was made when Bert Franklin, employed in the capacity of investigator by the defense, endeavored to "get to" the jury.

Bribery had been attempted almost every day with witnesses, but we had amply protected our lines from such encroachments. Our most important witnesses were never left alone and in the case of Frank Eckhoff we saw to it that not even his wife and mother could reach him. Those witnesses who had been threatened with death after they had refused bribes were provided with guards.

District Attorney Fredericks and his force kept their eyes keen for an attempt to get jurors and when George N. Lockwood, a talesman, was approached by Franklin and given $500 in advance with a guarantee of $3,500 after the trial, the plot to fix this talesman was nipped in the bud. The second attempt was made with Robert Bain, an actual member of the McNamara jury. Bain swore that Franklin gave him $500 and promised $3,600 after the trial if he stood out for not guilty. Franklin was arrested for the Bain bribery and that was the final blow. The McNamaras would have to face twelve unbribed men for trial and the McNamaras and their counsel knew what witnesses we had and had a good idea of the testimony we would present. Both men would be found guilty of murder in the first degree and both would go to the gallows.

Panic hit the hearts of everyone connected with the effort to save these two murderers and the murderers themselves felt the rope tightening about their necks. Negotiations to save them from death on the gallows were opened. The first proposition made to Captain Fredericks was that J. B. McNamara plead guilty to murder in the first degree and be given any sentence save that of death and that J. J. McNamara be allowed to go free.

The district attorney was not content to see the weakling tool suffer for the man higher up and he declined the offer. Next came the same offer in writing only with the words, "save the sentence of death" scratched out with a pencil. The defense was willing to swing Jim if by conceding this miserable life to the law J. J. might be saved. The district attorney declined.

Finally the defense made the proposition that J. B. would plead guilty to the Los Angeles Times job and its twenty-one murders and J. J. would plead guilty to the Llewellyn Iron Works job.

Judge Boardwell accepted these pleas and sentenced J. B. to San Quentin for life and J. J. for fifteen years.

Judge Boardwell, in sentencing the two men, declared that they were murderers at heart and deserved the extreme penalty of the law. To J. B. McNamara the judge said:

"There is very little or no ray of comfort in the assertion that you did not intend to destroy life. The widows and orphans and the bereaved parents will look upon that statement at this time as a mockery. The circumstances are against you in making any such claim. A man who would put sixteen sticks of dynamite in a building full of combustible material, and I have in mind the paper which you must have known was scattered in enormous quantities throughout the building—I say that a man who under such circumstances could place a dynamite charge of that quantity in such a building, in which you as a printer knew that gas was burning in many places, and in which you knew there were scores of human beings toiling, must have had no regard whatever for the loss of his fellow human beings. He must have been a murderer at heart."

Now what did Clarence Darrow have to say in his statement to the public after the sentencing of his two clients, the two men who were held up to the people of the United States as two spotlessly innocent men who were being sacrificed by Capital through the agency of William J. Burns?

The two men were sentenced on December 5th, 1911. On that day Darrow said for publication in the Los Angeles Times, the paper which had risen from the wreck into which it had been cast by the dynamite of his clients:

"I have been here six months and spent many troubled days and sleepless nights trying to run down every clue and make every possible investigation; trying to do the best I could for my clients and the cause that I served. I had able associates who gave me their best effort and their best services through it all.

"From the first THERE WAS NEVER THE SLIGHTEST CHANCE TO WIN. To those who say it would have been better to have gone to trial and suffer complete defeat, I would call attention to the fact that there were thirty or forty hotel registers, three in Los Angeles, many in San Francisco and others in different parts of the country. There were scores of witnesses to identify J. B. Mc-, Namara as being present practically on the very day, and one, at least, in the building. There was overwhelming evidence of all kinds which no one could have surmounted if they would.

"If the State had put on its case we could not even put the defendant on the stand to deny the facts. We could not prove an alibi. We could not

prove he was not here. The failure to do so would
have been as much of an admission as it was to-day.
We were confronted with the situation of dragging
our case, perhaps for years, with NOTHING BUT
THE GALLOWS AT THE END and no chance
to raise any doubt in a thinking mind, and in the
meantime collecting money from thousands of people who could not know the facts.

"To go on under such circumstances would have
been madness and only postpone an evil until it
would have been a still greater evil and the consequences graver than they are now. All of this was
thoroughly understood by my associates and no one
hesitated about accepting it. We acted as we
thought right and best and will take the consequences of the act."

Near $200,000 were spent for the lawyers in
Los Angeles to find out that "there wasn't a chance
from the first" for the two men we had brought to
trial. A great deal more money was collected, the
poor, sweating, gullible workingman and working-
woman giving up with each call from their false
leaders and putting their money in his hands to dis-
pose of for them in the belief that what he was telling them was true. Even Darrow admitted that it
was not right to keep up the gouge.

CHAPTER XLVI

THE MYSTERY OF TWO LOST MEN

With the McNamaras disposed of, I immediately started the roundup of those gentlemen who had gathered with J. J. McNamara in the headquarters of the union in Indianapolis to await the reports from J. B. and McManigal as they made their tour with dynamite—that last tour when they started out with my operatives thick as bees at their heels.

We had a great mass of evidence to show that President F. M. Ryan and the rest of the officers of the International had shared in the masked war. This evidence we turned over to United States District Attorney Miller in Indianapolis and we brought along McManigal from Los Angeles as a witness against the conspirators. Nearly the entire executive body of the International was guilty of participating in the conspiracy of destruction and when we made the roundup the net brought forty-five ironworkers to the bar of justice. Thirty-eight were found guilty and sentenced to the Federal prison for terms of from one to seven years.

Tveitmoe and Clancy and Jack Munsey and the

other fattened parasites of the union were sent to Leavenworth prison to work for their keep behind bars. They no longer draw fat salaries and emergency sums from the union's deflated treasury.

With the beginning of the year 1913 we left the field of investigation for the many other tasks ahead of us. The structural ironworkers were rid of their grafters, crooks and murderers. They had a new slate before them.

In all this record which I have put down for the lasting chronicle of a serious warfare against Society and its laws there stands out to my eyes a most gratifying thing. My organization worked superbly and although private detective agencies are too frequently used for harboring crooks and professional blackmailers my men worked with clean hands as well as remarkably quick wits. Some of them sacrificed all of the comforts of life at times in order to do their work well, none of them succumbed to offers of big bribes and it is with genuine pride that I say that without their efficient aid and their fine integrity the success of my agency would never have been achieved.

Of the two Anarchists, Schmidt and Caplan, supplied to help J. B. McNamara in the destruction of the Times Building, all that can be said is that they are yet to be captured and to be made to answer to the charge of murder.

Among the many letters received by me to the effect that I would pay with my life for my share in the investigation one was signed by a man who declared himself to be Schmidt. He promises to come back to this country after his period of hiding abroad. He declared that he would return in order to murder me. If he is really living he may not be surprised if at any moment a hand closes on his shoulder and he finds himself a prisoner.

Caplan's wife was smuggled out of San Francisco by Tveitmoe and his assistants. But we had no charge against her. It is her husband who may yet look up at the gallows tree. It has been suggested that these two Anarchists were put away for fear that they would weaken and testify against the real conspirators in order to save their lives. We know nothing that would give us reason to believe that such a double murder was committed but in closing I shall quote from a letter written by a woman, evidently an Anarchist, in which she graphically suggests this solution of the disappearance of the two men.

Here it is:

"I went to Carmel Mission and a fruit ranch near there about the middle of October after the dynamiting of the Times Building.

"Followed the Carmel River up in the Flats and went to a house where lived a woman of stout build and a small-sized man.

"Was sent there by an old German priest of Carmel.

"Had some conversation with the woman and the man left.

"Was joined afterward by Schmidt and the boy of the Huber family. All were lodged in a camp up in Carmel mountain. About November 19th, there was war in the camp—a tragedy had taken place.

"The camp had been dynamited, how or by whom I do not know. A man on horseback went there hunting. While he was there, it is my belief, two persons were dynamited, their bodies rolled in t paulin with stone sinkers, and thrown into Carmel River to pass along the coast in the undertow north above Santa Cruz.

"On the eighth of February I had a very strong feeling that these bodies in tarpaulin were passing Point of Pines. I went out there and at the spot indicated there was an unusually large number of gulls incessantly brooding over the drift and they did not leave until the tide turned."

Whether that was the last of Caplan or not I do not know.

FINIS